Buil[illegible]s Recognition

Alan Hollingsworth

First published 1987

086364 038 9

Published by Ian Allan Ltd, Shepperton, Surrey; and printed by Ian Allan Printing Ltd at their works at Coombelands in Runnymede, England

Published in the United States by

HIPPOCRENE BOOKS, Inc.,
171 Madison Avenue,
New York, N.Y.10016

Front cover, top left:
Ashdown Park, Berkshire, c1660.

Front cover, top right:
St Eadburga, Broadway, H&W, Norman & C14.

Front cover, bottom left
Castle Howard, North Yorks, c1705.

Front cover, bottom right:
Clarence Square, Cheltenham, Glos, c1832.

Back cover, top:
Chedington Court, Dorset c1890, a return to the Jacobean vernacular and carefully done. Chedington is now an hotel.

Back cover, bottom:
St Peter & St Paul, Albury, Surrey. A Saxon church given a cupola in the 17th century and restored by Pugin c1839 who put in the quarterfoiled five-light plate tracery window.

Contents

Glossary — A Few New Words?

Like all specialist subjects, architecture has a language of its own and although I have endeavoured throughout this book to keep the use of technical words and phrases to a minimum, the use of some of the better known terms is unavoidable. (As was once said of the 'yorker' in cricket, it is difficult to see how some parts of buildings could be called "owt else'.)

In the pages that follow the main characteristics of each building type are examined under various headings, the main ones being: *plan* — how it is laid out on the ground; *elevation and walling* — how it looks in profile and what its walls are made of; *roof* — the shape and the material used; *windows and doors* — the shape of the openings and their position in the walls and the pattern of the glazing of the windows; *chimneys* — their position and the shape of the shaft. The following paragraphs illustrate some of the technical expressions used later in the text.

Plans

Church plans — Most (but not all) pre-Reformation (ie earlier than the 16th century) churches are aligned east to west with the altar at the eastern end. Fig 1 shows the main parts of a typical church plan as it evolved from Saxon times onwards.

Castle plans — Castles were usually sited in commanding positions (like Windsor on a bluff over the Thames) and aligned to place the keep in the best defensive location. Fig 2 shows the parts of a general plan of a medieval castle.

House plans — Houses tend to be aligned in relation to adjacent roads or streets but some very grand houses are aligned to an axis appropriate to their position in the landscape — and not always facing south. Plans of detached houses varied as they increased in size and complexity from Norman times onwards. Fig 3 shows the plan of a typical medieval manor house from which many later types evolved.

Elevation and walling

Elevation — The elevation of a building is its vertical aspect, face or facade. There are various points to note: the number of floors or storeys, the height of the eaves or parapet, whether the wall has buttresses or columns, the position of and shape of windows (known as the fenestration) and doors, the shape of gables, towers and turrets, decorations like pinnacles and balustrades, etc. Fig 4 shows a church elevation; Fig 5 one of the medieval manor house; Fig 6 one of a classical house. Gables are useful indicators of style and period. Fig 7 shows examples.

Walling — Different materials are used for the walls of buildings — stone, brick, timber, flint — either solely or as mixtures. When stones — or flints — are used as they come this is called 'random rubble'; if they are sized and laid in layers or courses the walling is 'coursed rubble'; if the stone is cut into neat blocks and fitted together with fine joints, it is called 'ashlar'. Fig 8

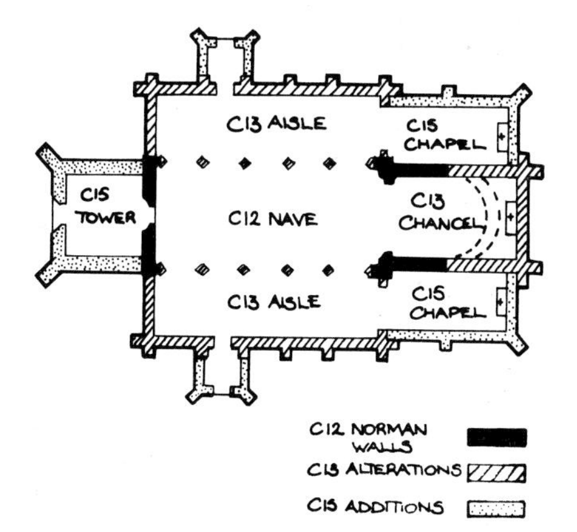

Fig 1
How parish churches evolved.
All drawings by Sandra Forty

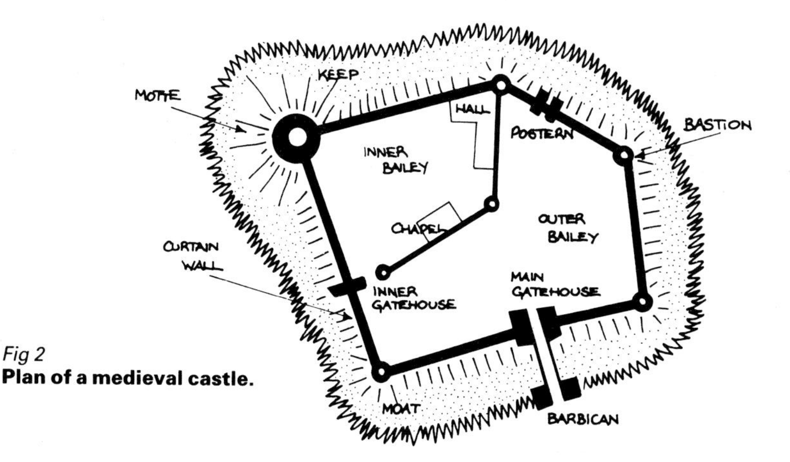

Fig 2
Plan of a medieval castle.

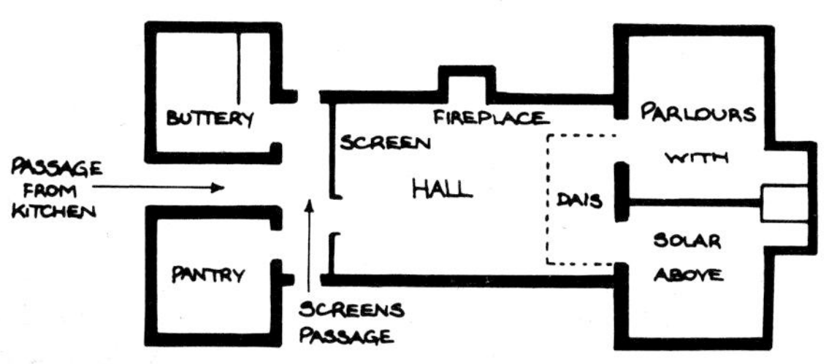

Fig 3
Plan of a medieval manor house.

1
7
2
3
4
6
5

4
1
2
3

Fig 4
A church elevation exemplified by Lavenham Church, Suffolk: 1 West tower with angle buttresses; 2 Nave with battlements; 3 Chancel; 4 South porch; 5 South aisle; 6 Chantry chapel; 7 Pinnacle.

Fig 5
A medieval hall house elevation — in this case King's House, Salisbury, Wiltshire. 1 Two-storey porch leading to screens passage; 2 Great hall with dormer gables above; 3 Mullioned and transomed windows (C16); 4 Solar and parlour wing refronted with bay windows (C16).

Fig 6
A classical house elevation, Marble Hill House, Twickenham, Middlesex: 1 Basement; 2 First (main) floor; 3 Attic storey; 4 Pediment.

shows some examples. In brickwork, the arrangement of bricks laid lengthwise — stretchers — and bricks laid end on — headers — goes to make up a pattern known as a 'bond', 'English Bond' and 'Flemish Bond' are the most frequently encountered.

Roofing

Roof shapes — The most common types of roof shape are shown in Fig 9: Pitched almost universal until the 17th century; Hipped, 17th century

Fig 7
Gable shapes: 1 Dormer; 2 Crow-stepped; 3 Dutch; 4 Shaped.

Fig 8
Walling: 1 Random rubble; 2 Coursed rubble; 3 Ashlar.

Fig 9
Roof shapes: 1 Pitched; 2 Hipped with gables; 3 Mansard.

onwards; Mansard, 18th century onwards. The shape and pitch — steepness of a roof — is to some extent determined by the material used for roofing.

Roofing materials — Thatch — reed, straw or heather — and small stone tiles require a pitch of 45° or more; slates and pantiles as low as 30°; heavy stone slabs about 35°. Lead is best for flat or very low pitch roofs because of creep.

Windows and Doors

Window types — Apart from the usual flat windows in walls there are the following types: Bay windows, which are canted projections rising from the ground; Bow windows are rounded projections; Oriel windows are usually rounded projections from an upper storey; Dormer windows are vertical windows in a sloping roof with their own roofs (see Fig 10). When windows can be opened vertically like doors they are casements; if they slide up and down, they are sash windows.

Fig 10
Window types: 1 Canted bay; 2 Bow; 3 Oriel; 4 Venetian.

Fig 11
Window shapes: 1 Norman; 2 Medieval; 3 Tudor; 4 Georgian; 5 Regency; 6 Victorian.

1

2

3

4

Fig 12

Doorcases: 1 Norman; 2 Medieval; 3 Tudor; 4 Jacobean; 5 Stuart; 6 Georgian; 7 Regency.

5 6 7

Window openings — The shape of the top of window openings usually is a major indicator of the style of the building — rounded for Romanesque, pointed for Gothic and flat or segmented for Classical. All but the earliest of windows are divided into lights by vertical mullions and horizontal transoms. Where these form a decorative pattern they are known as tracery. When the glass is held in small panes by lead channels, these are, of course, leaded lights; where it is held by wooden mouldings, these are the glazing bars. Fig 11 shows some examples of window types.

Door openings and Doorcases — Like window openings, these again reflect the style of the building but often have more decorative surrounds — architraves — than window openings. Door heads especially indicate style and period. Fig 12 shows some examples. Doors themselves quite frequently reflect the style of panelling used at a particular period.

Chimneys

Chimney Stack — The external and visible structure of brick or masonry that contains the flues from several fireplaces; if there is only one flue it is a chimney shaft. The chimney cap is the moulded or ornamental finish to a chimney stack but does not include the chimney pot (not introduced until the late 18th century). Chimney-piece is an old name for what we now call a fireplace.

General Introduction

Those of us who live in the British Isles have a heritage of buildings that is remarkably rich and varied and one that runs down to us in an almost unbroken stream from Anglo-Saxon times to the present day. Each and every building whether great or small, intact or in ruins has something to tell us about the people who originally built it and, in many cases, those who have lived in it since. This great heritage is, in effect, the story of England, Scotland and Wales told not in words but in stone, in timber and in brick. To read, understand and enjoy that story to the full means rather more than simply enjoying looking at old buildings, pleasurable though that may be in itself. It requires at least a basic knowledge of the various building styles as they have evolved over the centuries and with it some grasp of the philosophical, social and technical factors that lay behind the original architectural design.

As with all such interests, a little understanding can grow into a greater knowledge, an initial interest into an absorbing pleasure. This book has therefore two purposes. The first is to provide some of the basic information required to be able to recognise and date the style of each of the main building types to be found throughout our towns, villages and countryside. The second is to provide notes on the means of acquiring a more detailed knowledge of a fascinating subject. There are also notes on the locations of buildings of the style and type described in each section but in a compact book of this sort, there is a limit to the numbers it is possible to include. I have also endeavoured wherever possible to give the locations of properties that are open to or accessible to the public either because they are in the hands of one of the preservation societies or are inns or hotels. Churches nowadays regrettably may not always be open, but they are nearly always accessible from the outside. As far as the bigger buildings are concerned, the annual guides published by the National Trust in England and its Scottish equivalent and by English Heritage, Cadw in Wales and Historic Buildings and Monuments in Scotland are invaluable. I also particularly recommend the annual publication *Historic Houses, Castles and Gardens Open to the Public* published by British Leisure Publications.

Let us first look at the main categories of building likely to be seen all around the country. We can group them into broad historic styles and functions — like 'Medieval Monastic' or 'Victorian Industrial' — but there are perhaps two broad general divisions to be borne in mind — 'dead' buildings and 'living' buildings. By this I mean buildings that have ceased to function in the role for which they were primarily designed on the one hand and buildings still in active use in their primary purpose as places of worship, grain stores or dwelling places on the other. Dead buildings can be in ruins like most of the abbeys and monasteries and many of the castles in the kingdom, and not a few country houses, barns and isolated cottages. Like other skeletons, they are architectural anatomical specimens. But dead buildings can also be artificially preserved like mummies and there is a whole range of these from carefully preserved monuments like Shakespeare's birthplace in Stratford or Brighton's gay Pavilion, to abbey churches turned into country houses like Mottisfont or any of the plethora of redundant churches and chapels now doing duty as private homes and tithe barns similarly converted. All too often such mummification removes and destroys the inside of an old building and permanently alters its exterior to fulfil its new role. Compared with this, living buildings for the greater part do tend like all living things to go on changing and usually growing. In this regard, there is absolutely nothing new in the modern fashion for home extensions. Throughout architectural history those who owned or occupied castles or cottages, who controlled cathedrals or chapels, worked farms or ran factories have altered and adapted their premises to suit the needs of the time whether to cope with growing families, expanding businesses or simply to impress their neighbours with their power, their piety, their wealth or their taste. And despite the often commendable activities of the preservationists, this is not a process that is likely to stop. Thus for the student and enthusiast for old buildings, the pure examples of a particular style are the exceptions rather than the rule although there are still plenty about and preservation has at least meant that more care and concern for style has gone into recent renovations. For the most part, however, surviving historic buildings still being used are likely to be mixtures of styles. One looks for the Tudor house behind the Georgian facade, the medieval church behind the Victorian 'Gothick', the real behind the make-believe. As I said in the beginning, supplying the means of acquiring a little of the knowledge to enjoy such architectural detective work is the main purpose of this book. Dead and alive buildings are likely to be found in all styles and all periods. Saxon churches are still very much alive where tower blocks erected as recently as the late sixties are unmistakably — and deservedly, some would say — dead. This is not to imply that all that is old is necessarily good. History has had many previous 'Ronan Points'. 'Jerry building' as a term dates from the 1830s — and Liverpool — at a time when the Greek revival was in full spate and English domestic architecture at its most elegant. History too is full of examples of superb Gothic church towers and steeples that collapsed and killed people and of architectural experiments that ended in failure. Again knowledge of the whys and wherefores of a building add to its charm — even if it has few others. What, for example, could be more fascinating than the philosophy behind follies? And who in the last century would ever have believed that in our times preservation orders have been put on Victorian work-houses?

There is one other broad division that is of relevance. This is the use of the words 'polite' and 'vernacular' to divide the two main streams of buildings into those which were built to predetermined plan or design and those which were erected in keeping with local practice and materials. The former is likely to have been subject to stylistic influences from outside the area and to have required the importation of either labour or materials. The one we might say in modern terms was 'designer' built, the other home-made although as with everything associated with a vast subject like this, there are many blurred edges and numerous buildings do not fall clearly into either category. Inevitably too, in a book about architectural styles, the emphasis is on the 'polite' rather than on the vernacular — the trend-setters rather than the trend followers. This is in no way to demean vernacular architecture which forms a far larger part of our heritage than does the 'polite'.

For the purposes of this book, I have divided the subject into three main eras — that of the Romanesque, the Gothic, and the Classical. I have then subdivided each of these eras into periods, relating each period to the reign of a particular monarch or series of monarchs.

I have done this largely because what is lost in accuracy is gained in convenience and this is not an architectural textbook but what I hope is a handy guide of use to the enthusiast rather than the expert. Each of the main styles has its own chapter and in the introduction I have discussed the philosophical, social and cultural background to buildings of the period — long words for saying how people who put up buildings thought at the time, how they felt and acted and what factors influenced them. I have then set out the main examples of each style and the main points to look out for. For those who want to learn more, in the bibliography on page 157 I have given a list of books suitable for further study and details of several societies active in the field of architectural history and its natural concomitant, preservation.

Most of the photographs in this book are my own and I must apologise at once to the photographic purists who will notice that many of the buildings appear to have lost several feet at their bases. All I have done is to remove the cars that clutter our streets. Apart from the obvious distraction they pose, the fact that they change their styles every other year whereas buildings change theirs only about every 50 years tends to make quite satisfactory architectural photographs appear dated. For the remainder of the photographs, I am most grateful to John Mackay of Lauder, Dr John Shannon of York, John Belheli of St Albans and Miss Francesca Barran of the National Trust for lending me prints. I am also most grateful to Lyndon Cave for allowing me to use drawings from his book *The Smaller English House*.

Alan Hollingsworth

Above right:
The Jew's House, The Strait, Lincoln. Still very much alive after 800 years, what might be called a 'redundant Norman bank' was built in c1175. Note the arches over the doorway and the two upper storey windows where the hall was. You can now have your lunch where the first owner kept his gold.

Right:
Minster Lovell Hall, Oxon. The evocative ruins of a medieval great house built c1431-42 and demolished in the 18th century. The house was built round three sides of a courtyard with the fourth side facing the River Windrush. Its ruins have been carefully preserved and catalogued by English Heritage and reveal clearly the anatomy of a large medieval house.

JEWS HOUSE

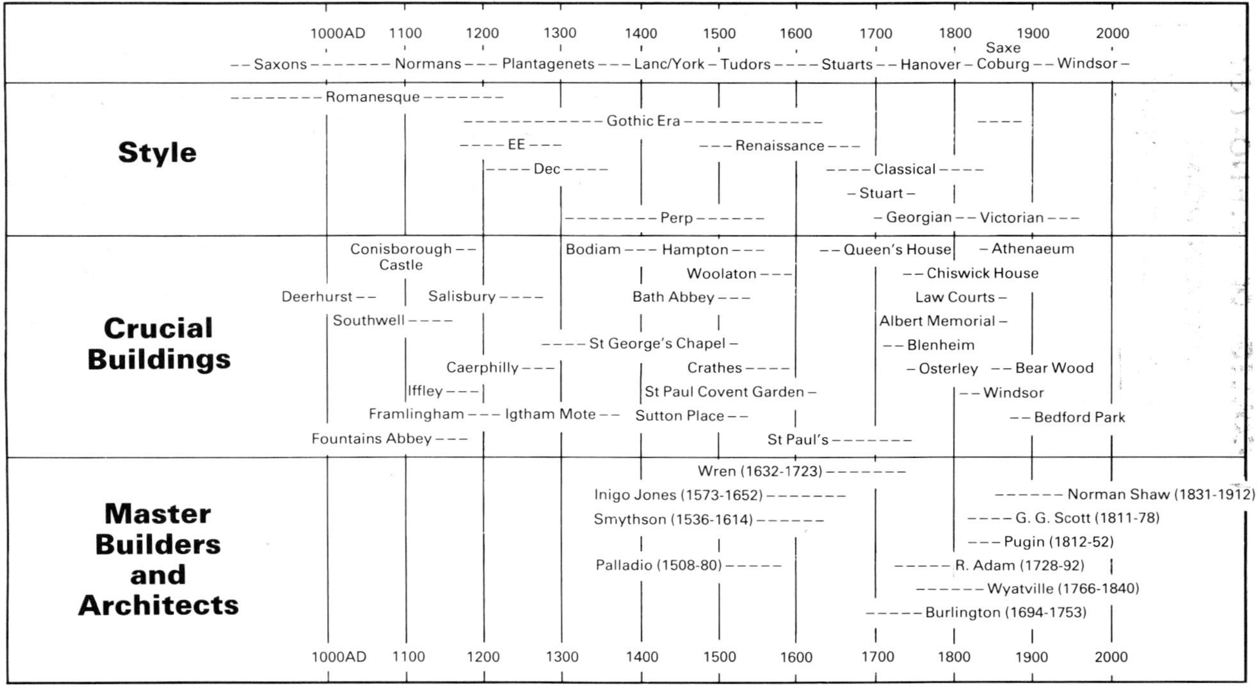

1000AD 1100 1200 1300 1400 1500 1600 1700 1800 1900 2000

-- Saxons ------- Normans --- Plantagenets --- Lanc/York – Tudors ---- Stuarts -- Hanover – Saxe Coburg -- Windsor –

Style

-------- Romanesque -------

------------ Gothic Era ------------ ----

----EE---

---- Dec ----

--- Renaissance ---

---- Classical ----

– Stuart –

-------- Perp ------

– Georgian -- Victorian ---

Crucial Buildings

Conisborough Castle --

Deerhurst --

Southwell ----

Salisbury ----

Caerphilly ---

Iffley ---

Framlingham --- Igtham Mote --

Fountains Abbey ---

Bodiam --- Hampton ---

Woolaton ---

Bath Abbey ---

---- St George's Chapel –

Crathes ----

St Paul Covent Garden –

Sutton Place --

St Paul's -------

-- Queen's House

– Athenaeum

-- Chiswick House

Law Courts –

Albert Memorial –

-- Blenheim

– Osterley

-- Bear Wood

-- Windsor

-- Bedford Park

Master Builders and Architects

Wren (1632-1723) -------

Inigo Jones (1573-1652) -------

Smythson (1536-1614) ------

Palladio (1508-80) -----

------ Norman Shaw (1831-1912)

---- G. G. Scott (1811-78)

--- Pugin (1812-52)

----- R. Adam (1728-92)

------ Wyatville (1766-1840)

----- Burlington (1694-1753)

1000AD 1100 1200 1300 1400 1500 1600 1700 1800 1900 2000

Fig 13
Historic building styles: The Romanesque, Gothic and Classical eras.

THE ROMANESQUE ERA, c600-1200

The Anglo-Saxon and Anglo-Norman Period, c800-1200

In terms of what little 'polite' architecture there was during this first evolutionary period, the main influence came from the recently defunct Roman Empire and is known as 'Romanesque' — in the manner of the Romans. The period began with the westward spread of Christianity into the pagan former colonies of Imperial Rome and ended with the Romanesque style being replaced with what we now call the 'Gothic'. And in the vernacular, the first glimmerings of an English traditional style began to make their appearance. The dates are, of course, no more than imprecise indicators of when changes took place. The process of such changes is invariably gradual and further blurring inevitably occurs at this historical distance and with the dearth of surviving records and buildings. Similarly, the distinction between 'Anglo-Saxon' and 'Anglo-Norman' is a very fine one. It is impossible to say when one starts and the other begins to within about half a century either way. In this regard the apparently seismic event of 1066 is but an incident in a process that had been in train for several generations.

The Roman Empire of which parts of Britain were an outpost until the early 5th century was a highly developed, largely urban society with its own distinctive architectural style and methods of building which it introduced into all the territories its armies occupied. Major buildings were of stone or brick although, especially in the countryside, the Romans also built in timber. Some Roman building has survived to the present day — for example, the Newport Arch in Lincoln and castle ruins at Porchester. Numerous villas have also been excavated, notably that at Fishbourne near Chichester. We also have substantial documentary records of the period to give us a clear idea of what the buildings looked like in their prime. Roman buildings are not however regarded as being in the mainstream of the evolution of British building styles because they were essentially imported in complete form, were subject to little local variation and fell into ruin when the importers left. On the other hand, as we shall see, the influence of the Roman style per se became extremely important in that evolution.

The mixture of Germanic peoples who occupied most of England and parts of Scotland after the Roman withdrawal and whom we usually know as 'Saxons' were far more primitive. They were tribal and agrarian with little need for large settlements like the cities the Romans had left behind and which early in their occupation, they were content to leave to what remained of the indigenous Romano-British population, seeing them superstitiously as 'the works of former giants'. The Saxons had a bardic rather than a literary tradition and until the 9th century and the first of the Anglo-Saxon chronicles, there were few written records. It is this absence of such written records from the 5th century until the 9th century that gives the period its title 'Dark Ages' among historians. Similarly, since the Saxons also built primarily in timber, no heritage of Saxon timber building has survived other than one or two rare bits of late Saxon carpentry discovered in later buildings and a plethora of archaeological sites with stone plinths and post holes emanating from the period. The early Saxon era is thus something of an architectural 'Dark Age' as well. Nonetheless, the later Saxons were responsible for the beginnings of what was to evolve into a national style in church building (see **Saxon Churches**). During the late Saxon period too the first examples of what was to become a pervasive and distinctive style of essentially English domestic vernacular architecture, the 'open hall' house, made their appearance. In its primitive form, the open hall house was a single-storied structure probably with timber walls — whole or split logs standing side by side, open to the rafters under a thatched roof. Such halls were the centres of Saxon settlements and served as meeting places (moot halls) and banqueting halls as well as homes for the local thanes.

Christianity had largely disappeared from mainland Britain after the Roman withdrawal but the faith had survived in Celtic Ireland to be taken back to Scotland by St Columba in 563AD from where it spread southwards into Northumbria. Through other missionaries — one of whom (St Piran) is said to have floated across on a millstone — the Celtic church also spread across the Irish Sea to Wales and Cornwall and into southwest England finding a focus in the Glastonbury region. Another mission, sent direct from Rome by Pope Gregory the Great, and led by a monk later to become the first Archbishop of Canterbury and a saint — Augustine — arrived in Kent in 597, converted the king of the Jutes, Aethelbert, and was given land to build a monastery. The significance of this from the architectural point of view is that Augustine brought with him other monks skilled in the building of masonry churches in the Roman tradition and these skills were passed on to converted Saxon communities who lived in areas where stone was readily available by quarrying or from the ruins of nearby Roman cities. In short, some 300 years or so after the Romans had left, their architectural heritage came back to Britain with the Christian church after it had by similar means also returned to Germany and France, including, of course, Normandy. However, the church building styles that came in with the returning Christian church were neither exclusively nor purely classical Graeco-Roman. The Holy Roman Empire at the time was divided between Italy and Byzantium (Constantinople) and the influence of the church building style of the Levant based on the three memorial temples built over Christianity's holiest shrines in Jerusalem and Bethlehem also reached as far west as Britain. But for the most part Saxon churches built over the succeeding centuries — and Domesday in 1085 records that there were several thousand — were of timber and in the same style as Saxon moot halls. (Only one of these has survived and that a late example — the nave of the church of Greenstead in Essex.) And even those later (c700) Saxon churches that were built of stone or reused Roman brick tended to look as though they had been built of timber. In Wales and Scotland, the Celtic church built simple crude chapels of wood and wattle with only a few in stone which excavations show to have been usually of two small rectangular rooms, the larger one, the nave, for the worshippers, the smaller, the chancel, for the priest and the altar. (See **Saxon Churches**.)

Above:
Newport Arch, Lincoln. The authentic shape of a Roman arch but a little short in the legs. This was once the north gate of Lindum Colonia but since that time the surface of the road has risen by about 8ft.

Right:
Chapter House Entrance, Winchester Cathedral. Not Roman but 'Romanesque'. Sir Nikolaus Pevsner calls this 'one of the mightiest pieces of early Norman architecture in the land'. Sturdy piers, big scalloped capitals. The house in the background is No 1 The Close, built in 1699.

In the centuries preceding the Conquest, the Saxons built cathedrals — perhaps as many as 15 — 'minsters' (we owe the word to them) and a variety of abbey churches, the last in the Benedictine tradition (see **Medieval Monasteries**), as well as many parish churches. The style in which they were built was usually Romanesque or Byzantine. The first copied the style of the Roman basilica — a long rectangular hall with two parallel lines of columns giving, in effect, a nave and two aisles. At the eastern end — both traditions aligned their churches towards Jerusalem, ie towards the east — was a semicircular extension or apse, containing the altar. The Byzantine style favoured a cruciform church around a central raised structure — the domes of the East giving way to capped or steepled towers in the West. These are, of course, the pure styles and were subject to a host of variations and amalgamations. (See **Saxon Churches**.)

The Viking — or Norse/Danish — invasion of the north and east of England in 871 and the long struggle that followed saw the destruction of many cathedrals — that at York, for example — abbeys and churches and the wholesale slaughter of priests, monks and nuns. The Vikings also attacked and destroyed churches and monasteries in both Scotland and Wales but did not settle in significant numbers. Christianity and the building of churches stood still in the disputed areas until at the peace of Wedmore, Alfred the Great brought about the conversion of the Danes but accepted their settlement of much of eastern England. Although the Danes did not make any clear contribution to architectural or building development, they reintroduced the concept of the township or borough as an administrative entity. In the struggles with the Saxons they made several former Roman walled cities — Lincoln, Nottingham, Leicester, Derby, Stamford — into boroughs and strengthened their defences by the building of ramparts and palisades. The idea was new to the Saxons but they later copied it, notably at Canterbury and in the Midlands, and strongholds and fortified towns made their appearance in England for the first time since the Romans had left. It seems unlikely however, that any of these fortifications were built in masonry — the castle at Corfe is a possible exception. Some Saxon thanes may also have fortified their halls with moats and earth ramparts but the building of 'castles' as such did not come until after the Conquest.

At the time of the early Viking excursions into eastern England, other Norse tribes had swept south through the Low Countries and had founded the kingdom of Normandy. Thus when William of Normandy came to take the throne of England he came to a land of which large areas had been occupied by his own race for many generations and where a specifically Norman influence was already strong. (The last 'English King', Edward the Confessor, had not only been bought up at the Norman court, his advisers, notably his bishops were all Normans. His Abbey Church of Westminster, consecrated the day before he died in 1066, was of Norman stone and was designed and built by Norman craftsmen.)

After their victory at Hastings and the subsequent campaign of subjection, the Normans had first of all to secure the boundaries of their new kingdom and hold the English down. Their solution was the building of a vast network of castles — eventually some 2,500 in England, Scotland and Wales. Although many of the early castles were of the timber and earth 'motte and bailey' type, those that protected the Welsh and Scottish marches and the main lines of communication around London — 200 in all — were soon rebuilt in stone. (See **Norman Castles**.) The second Norman objective was to strengthen the hold of the Christian church in its Roman rather than its Celtic form over the English population and bring the subject people into conformity with Norman custom. For this William and his bishops — in those days feudal bishops like feudal barons were powerful landowners, some even built castles — initiated a great monastic revival with the building of huge cathedrals, abbeys and churches throughout the land. They ruthlessly swept aside the Saxon cathedrals, minsters and abbey churches declaiming their builders to be *rudes et idiotas* (boors and blockheads). (See **Norman Cathedrals, Norman Churches**.) The century that followed the Conquest was thus one of enormous building achievement. Indeed the building of so many magnificent castles, cathedrals and churches has been rightly described as one of the wonders of the medieval age. Although they must have used much indigenous labour in their vast building programme, the Normans themselves provided the inspiration, the resources and the skilled management and design. Paramount in this process was the influence of a new class of highly skilled master-masons, the architects of the time, and for the most part, totally anonymous although many of their works have survived a millenium. The style was, as we have seen, still Romanesque — strong and simple, thick walls, massive columns, semicircular arches, decoration confined to chevron moulding and occasional simple carving of capitals of columns. By the middle of the 12th century, however, the sculptors rather than the masons initiated an era of change with more elaborate decoration that led into the steady transition from Norman to Gothic. But, although by the 12th century Normans were beginning to think of themselves as English, none of them would have recognised the term 'Gothic' with which we nowadays distinguish the next period of architecture. It was to be coined in faraway Italy at the time of the Renaissance, two centuries later.

Saxon Churches

There is only one survivor of a host of Saxon churches built of timber, that at Greenstead in Essex built 1035. (There are also two other timber churches in Essex, at Stock and West Hanningfield which, although of a later date (14th century) are similar to late Saxon wooden churches based on the Byzantine model.) Of Saxon cathedrals, minsters and abbey churches only remnants of crypts and foundations are to be found in later buildings, eg at York and Canterbury. There are however, said to be some 400 parish churches with visible Saxon work but among these unadulterated and complete Saxon churches are very rare — and for obvious reasons. Those that have survived are invariably small, simple and often crude in structure. Their main characteristics can be summarised as follows:

Plans

Rectangular nave and chancel on the Celtic model. Some have a rounded apse at the east end of the chancel. Some western bell towers were added later, c1000.

Aisled nave with internal piers or pillars. Smaller un-aisled chancel.

Cross-shaped with a strong central tower, short wings to the tower as side chapels or porches north and south. The chancel is often apsed to the east. The nave was often extended to the west.

Axial with a central tower between the nave and the chancel but without north-south wings or transepts.

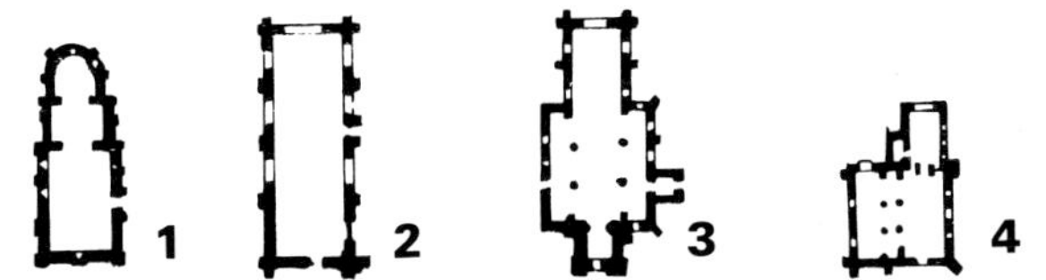

Fig 14
Saxon and Norman parish church plans: 1 Apsidal; 2 Aisleless; 3 Aisled nave north and south; 4 Irregular aisled.

Elevation and Walling

Tall thick plain walls with a few small openings, usually built of random rubble — rough stones of various shapes and sizes — ashlar — cut blocks with fine joints — is very rare at this period. Long and short work quoins are a feature (corners with heavy stones laid alternately upright and flat). Later churches have herring-bone pattern stonework, blind arcading and frequent use of pilaster strips called 'lesenes' — long thin stones let into the face of the wall — in a criss-cross pattern.

Roofing

No Saxon roofing has survived. It was probably mostly thatch. There is some

variety in the roofing of towers — saddle-back, Rhenish helm, cruciform and broach spire.

Windows and Doors
Small and few. Windows are usually single with round arches or with a simple triangle of stones above as in a timber building. Wider openings like bell-cotes are often double arched with a distinctive central baluster shaped pillar.

Exterior
Very plain and simple with rough stone often exposed. Little carving.

Locations

Scotland:

Celtic remains only. **Brechin**, Tayside, round tower c1000; **Restenneth**, Tayside, square tower c700.

England:

North — **Bolam**, Northumberland, church tower c1050; **Escomb**, Co Durham, church c680; **Morland**, Cumbria, church tower c1060; **Heysham**, Lancashire, monastery remains and church c850.

Midlands — **Barrow**, Salop, church c1040; **Repton**, Derbyshire, church c800; **Stow**, Lincolnshire, church c1010; **Barnack**, Cambridgeshire, church tower c1020.

South — **Sompting**, West Sussex, church c1040; **Worth**, West Sussex, church c1030; **Wickham**, Berkshire, church tower c1020; **Breamore**, Hampshire, church c1010.

Southwest — **Bradford on Avon**, Wiltshire, church c700; **St Piran in Sabulo**, near Newquay, Cornwall, chapel c600.

Left:
Odda's Chapel, Deerhurst, Gloucestershire. Comprising a small rectangular nave and a tiny rectangular chancel, this Saxon chapel is one of the most complete now surviving and can be authentically dated at 1056. Its existence was unsuspected for centuries until it was discovered as part of the adjoining half-timbered house in 1885. Note the round-headed window opening.

Above:
St Mary, Breamore, Hampshire. This was a Saxon cruciform church built about 1000. Its main surviving Saxon features are the central tower and the south transept. Notice the shape of the windows and doorways in the transept and the characteristic 'long and short work' of the quoins.

Right:
St Laurence, Bradford on Avon, Wiltshire. Another Saxon church that was not discovered until the 19th century — in 1856 after the nave had been used as a school and the chancel as a cottage. Its date of building has not been resolved but it is probably late-Saxon. Note the blank arcading. The church is unusual that it is aligned ENE.

Norman Castles

The Norman Conquest in which barely more than 10,000 invaders were able to overcome and occupy a country of some two million warlike people was a military achievement of the first magnitude. It came about because the Normans had an insurmountable advantage over the Saxons in contemporary military technology — armoured cavalry and castles — above all, castles. William even brought a portable wooden 'castle' across the Channel with him and erected it at Pevensey on the eve of the Battle of Hastings in 1066. And after his victory there, he very quickly built other castles, notably at Dover, to safeguard his lines of communication with Normandy.

These early castles were of what is known as the 'motte and bailey' type — a man-made mound of earth usually standing within an oval 'bailey' surrounded by a ditch or moat and other earthworks and a strong timber palisade. On top of the motte — or some strategic rock or cliff — was built the keep or donjohn (from whence comes the word 'dungeon'). At first these keeps were also of timber but not long after the Conquest, many of the more important ones were rebuilt in stone. During the reigns of the first three Norman kings, castle-building was strictly controlled and required a royal licence. Probably about 1,000 were built up to 1135. Thereafter, in the troubled times of Stephen's reign (1135-54), there was a spate of private or 'adulterine' (ie unlicensed) castle building and as many as another 1,100 may

Above:
Conisborough Castle, South Yorkshire. This is a hall-keep castle with a buttressed circular keep about 90ft (27m) high. The only entrance is on the first floor where the walls are 15ft (4.5m) thick. The ground floor is an undercroft, domed and windowless; it can be reached only by ladder from the first floor. The hall is on the second floor, the solar and chapel are on the third with the guardroom on the top floor.

have been built. For in those days, he who held the castle controlled the land and though the Normans were good at building castles they were no better than their opponents at dealing quickly with castles that had fallen into the wrong hands. (Until gunpowder arrived in the 14th century, prolonged siege and starvation were the only effective weapons.) Order was restored under Henry II (1154-89) and castle building was strictly licensed again.

The first Norman castles had a purely military function although even they had to accommodate a garrison and sustain it if necessary throughout a long siege. Later castles were not only controlling strongpoints, they were also the homes of rich landowners who possessed a taste for as much comfort as the times afforded and for impressing their neighbours with their culture and wealth. Thus the long struggle between the needs of security and domesticity in castle-building began. Other influences were also at work. Norman England was still part-Continental and ideas and events in Europe affected castle design here just as, later in the period, experience on the Crusades brought in new designs from the Islamic world. We also see the emergence of the skilled master mason or 'ingeniator' as a designer of castles: Gundulf, Bishop of Rochester who built the White Tower from which the Tower of London takes its name, as well as Colchester; Alnoth who built Orford; Bigod who built Framlingham in Suffolk.

As with Norman churches and cathedrals, many castles of Norman origin have been altered and rebuilt over the centuries. Nonetheless, despite the deliberate ruination perpetrated by Cromwellian forces after the English Civil War, substantial examples of early Norman military architecture are still to be found throughout England and Wales.

There are three main types of Norman castle: the 'hall-keep' type, the 'shell-keep' type, and late in the period, castles that had high, fortified curtain walls, without keeps.

HALL-KEEP

Plan: Rectangular sometimes with corner turrets, octagonal or round, some earlier examples have buttresses. Multi-storied — well and storage in the basement, a two-storey hall above, and private chambers including the chapel at the top.

Elevation and Walling: Walls 15ft (5m) thick, thicker at the base (the batter), 90ft (27m) high. Solid stone or flint, coursed sometimes ashlared.

Windows and Doors: Small, crossbow slits only in the lower storeys. Single entrance through a small door high in the wall.

SHELL-KEEP

Plan: Circular or oval walling, open courtyard in the centre with a walkway along the top of the wall behind the battlements. Single entrance. Timber buildings built against the walls for use in times of siege. Other buildings — hall, solars, chapels etc, built in the bailey outside the keep but inside the curtain wall for peacetime use.

Elevation and Walling: Walls 7-10ft thick above a thicker batter, 20-30ft high.

Windows and Doors: The entrance doorway is protected by a gatetower. Few windows, mostly cross-bow slits only.

FORTIFIED CURTAIN WALL

Plan: Usually rectangular. The curtain wall is reinforced with many tall strong towers: at the corners and at intervals along the walls, and are doubled at the gateway. Courtyards (wards or baileys) are separated by other strong walling and contain the domestic buildings.

Elevation and Walling: Walls are 15-20ft thick, 35-40ft high. There is a walkway along the top of the wall behind the battlements.

Windows and Doors: Small and round-arched, mostly cross-bow slits. (This design was adopted from the Levant and employed widely during the medieval period. See **Medieval Castles**.)

Locations

Scotland:

There are no Norman castles in Scotland but the curtain-walled **Castle Roy**, Highlands, and **Castle Sween**, Strathclyde, with its hall-keep are Norman in style but built by local chieftains.

Wales:

Bronllys, near Brecon, Powys, circular hall-keep; **Pembroke**, Dyfed, circular hall-keep but also fortified curtain wall of Norman date; **Cardiff**, South Glamorgan, preserved Norman motte and shell-keep.

England:

North — **Bamburgh**, Northumberland, hall-keep (still occupied); **Brougham**, Cumbria, rectangular hall-keep (EH); **Barnard Castle**, County Durham, round hall-keep (EH); **Richmond**, North Yorkshire, rectangular hall-keep, some curtain walling.

Midlands — **Lincoln**, shell-keep and two Norman gateways;

Above left:
The Round Tower, Windsor Castle, Berkshire. The best known shell-keep in Britain — perhaps in the world — standing on a motte and with a moat round it (now dry). The lower part dates from c1150 and is not quite circular. It would have had only lightly-constructed timber buildings inside it. These were rebuilt c1360 and are still there. The tower itself was remodelled first in the time of Charles II(1649-85) and more drastically by Wyatville in the 1820s. He added 33ft (10m) and the machicolations.

Above:
Framlingham Castle. When built c1190-1210 this was the first of a new generation of castles without central keeps but with curtain walls reinforced by strong towers — Framlingham has 13 of them — reflecting lessons learnt on the Crusades. (The chimneys on the towers were added in early Tudor times.) *John Bethell*

Conisborough, South Yorkshire, round hall-keep with buttresses, curtain wall (EH); **Peveril**, Derbyshire, square hall-keep and gatehouse (EH); **Kenilworth**, Warkwickshire, square hall-keep with angle turrets (EH).

East Anglia — **Norwich**, Norfolk rectangular hall-keep; **Framlingham**, Suffolk, no keep, fortified curtain wall (EH).

Southeast — **Castle Hedingham**, Essex, square hall-keep; **Rochester**, Kent, tremendous hall-keep (EH); **Pevensey**, East Sussex, square Norman hall-keep, Roman curtain walling (EH); **Chilham**, Kent, tall octagonal keep with stair turrets.

South — **Windsor**, Berkshire, lower part of Round Tower is Norman shell-keep; **Odiham**, Hampshire, octagonal hall-keep; **Porchester**, Hampshire, large stone hall-keep inside a 4th century Roman brick fort (EH); **Carisbrooke**, IoW, shell-keep and curtain wall (EH).

Southwest — **Corfe**, Dorset, hall-keep and bailey wall (NT); **Totnes**, Devon, shell-keep on motte (EH); **Restormel**, near Lostwithiel, Cornwall, shell-keep (EH); **Tintagel**, Cornwall, gatehouse and hall (EH).

Norman Cathedrals

The God of the early Normans was austere, grim and above all, disciplined. So too were the great cathedrals and abbey churches they built to His glory in such vast numbers immediately after the Conquest. Not for them the architectural embellishments of the late Saxon period or the blandishments of the Byzantine tradition. William I was totally loyal to the Pope in Rome and the early Norman building style was Romanesque in its purest and simplest form — rounded classic columns or piers, rounded arches, little ornament or decoration. Later, by the middle of the 12th century, decoration of both piers and arches became more general and sculpture and carving made their appearance. Slowly too, the round arch gave way to the pointed one as the Anglo-Norman period began its transition into the Gothic 'Early English' (see **Medieval Cathedrals** and **Churches**).

The great programme of cathedral and abbey church building began within five years of Hastings with Canterbury and Rochester, Lincoln was begun in 1076. In many cases these great churches served a dual purpose — a priory church was the cathedral of the diocese and the priory officers served the cathedral. This was the case at Bristol, Carlisle, Canterbury, Chester, Durham, Ely, Norwich, Oxford, Peterborough, Rochester, Winchester and Worcester. Cathedrals were also built in Wales — Llandaff, Bangor, St Davids, St Asaph. In Scotland, King David I (1124-53) built three great churches in the Norman style at Jedburgh Abbey, St Andrews and Kelso.

Building to the greater glory of God was to remain a prime motivation of kings and bishops for a further three centuries and in consequence many of the original Norman cathedrals have been much altered by later building. Indeed some of them — Canterbury and Lincoln, for example, had substantial rebuilding in the 12th century. There was also the enduring hazard of fire. The Norman masons had not yet mastered the art of throwing a stone vault over a structure as big as a cathedral nave and roofs were all of timber. Their vulnerability to lightning strikes was demonstrated again as recently as 1983 at York Minster — and there were no lightning conductors in Norman times either. Nonetheless, there are still many examples of the Norman cathedral design to be found up and down the country.

Of the cathedrals the Normans built, only two have completely disappeared — that at Old Sarum and Old St Pauls in London. In addition, many of their larger abbey churches like Southwell and St Albans have subsequently become cathedrals, others like Romsey and Tewkesbury have survived as parish churches with cathedral dimensions. Many Norman cathedrals have after further rebuilding, subsequently become outstanding examples of later styles of ecclesiastical architecture and will be covered in later chapters.

The main characteristics of Norman cathedrals or great abbey churches can be summarised as follows although there is a great deal of local variation. Cathedrals in the north tend, for example, to be more massive and austere than those in the south designed to serve as fortresses if necessary.

Fig 15
Plan of Southwell Cathedral.

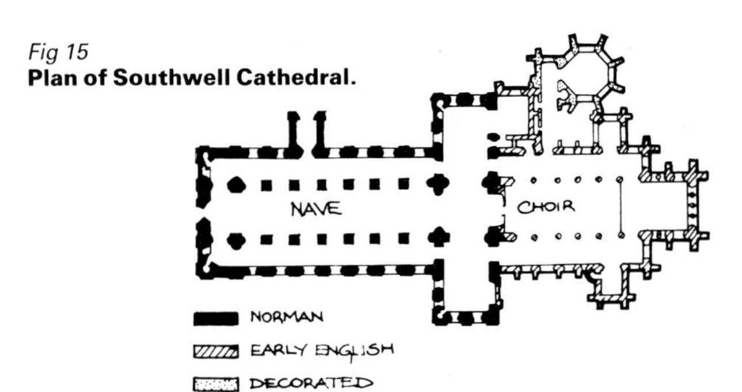

Above:
Southwell Minster, Nottinghamshire. Formerly an abbey church now a cathedral, the minster was begun in 1108 and is an excellent example of the austere and disciplined style of the Normans. The choir and the chapter house are medieval but the towers, transepts and nave — all seen here — are Norman. Points to note are: 1 The squat crossing tower with its round-headed blind arcading; 2 The three-storied chancel and transept with their flat buttresses and thick walls; 3 The small round-headed and colonetted window openings, the unusual round windows of the clerestory and the frilly corbel table under the eaves; 4 The severe west towers with their slit windows. The pyramidical caps were rebuilt in 1880 but are probably similar to those the Normans would have put on all three towers; 5 The west window is 15th century; 6 The great west portal has five orders of columns and decorated with zig-zag.

Plan: Cruciform with a short choir at the east ending in an apse or apses, deep transepts, and a long, aisled nave (520ft (159m) is not uncommon). A low tower over the crossing, twin towers at the west end.

Elevation and Walling: Three-storeyed (sometimes four if the crypt is counted). The nave arcade is the same height as the aisles, the 'triforium' or blind storey above corresponding in height to the slope of the aisle roof, and above that, the clerestory — a row of arched windows to light the nave or choir. Walls are sometimes as much as 10ft (3m) thick, stone facings with rubble infill. Saxon and roman material is sometimes reused. Shallow flat buttresses. Norman foundations were sometimes inadequate. Early Norman aisle and crossing 'drum' piers were tall and plain under round arches, thick squared off bases, plain capitals. Later in the period, arches, piers and capitals were decorated with incised carving — chevron (zig-zag) or diamond pattern. Some capitals were carved with mythical beasts, devils, monsters, human figures, plaitwork, etc. Internal blind arcading is a common decorative feature.

Windows and Doorways: Doorways are small, columned and round-headed. The arch is often filled with semi-circular stone (tympanum), and heavily carved. Arches and columns are often decorated. Windows, small, narrow and round-headed, often have two lights with a squat central pillar like a Saxon baluster.

Towers: Short and squat, like William I, and often resemble keeps. They are usually decorated by panelling or blind arcading and window slits. Originally they had low pyramid steeples.

West Fronts: A particular feature is for decorative carvings of saints, etc.

Locations

The following are still substantially Norman cathedrals.

Scotland:

St Andrews, Fife, cathedral ruins (1160-1318); **Dunblane**, Central Region, cathedral tower, c1130; **Restenneth**, Tayside, priory church tower, c1100; **Kirkwall**, Orkney, cathedral, c1137-80.

Wales:

St David's, Dyfed, cathedral nave, c1180.

England:

North — **Durham**, cathedral (1093-1175), the least altered in Britain, stone vaulting, first pointed arch; **Selby**, North Yorkshire, abbey church, c1100-80.

Midlands — **Blythe**, Nottinghamshire, priory church, early Norman nave, c1090; **Peterborough**, Cambridgeshire, cathedral, transept and nave, 1118-1200; **Southwell**, Nottinghamshire, minster, Norman nave transepts crossing and west towers, 1108-50; **Oxford**, former abbey church in Tom Quad, Christ Church, lower parts of nave, crossing and tower are Norman, 1158-1185; **Gloucester**, cathedral, crypt, nave and ambulatory, 1089-1150;

Tewkesbury, Gloucestershire, Norman abbey church, 1087-1121; **Hereford**, cathedral, 1080-1145.

East Anglia — **Norwich**, Norfolk, cathedral, a glorious Norman cathedral akin to Durham (1096-1150); **Ely**, Cambridgeshire, cathedral, Norman from crossing westwards (1083-1190); **Waltham Holy Cross**, Essex, abbey church, Norman nave, c1120. **St Albans**, Hertfordshire, Norman abbey church (now a cathedral), virtually complete, built on flint and reused Roman brick from Verulamium.

Southwest — **Exeter**, Devon, cathedral, Norman towers on transepts, c1170.

Southeast — **Rochester**, Kent, cathedral, 1077-1150; **Chichester**, West Sussex, cathedral, choir, nave and transepts, 1091-1140 and after fire, 1187-99; **Romsey**, Hampshire, late Norman abbey church of particular beauty, 1120-1200; **St Cross**, Winchester, Hampshire, monastic church in Norman transitional style with both round and pointed arches, c1200.

Below left:
St Machar's Cathedral, Aberdeen. It may look a little like Southwell and Norman but in fact it is mainly 15th century. Here the severity and discipline is imposed by the intractability of granite as a building stone.
John Mackay

Below right:
Northwest Tower, Chichester Cathedral, West Sussex. Built c1100, the cathedral was damaged by fire in 1187 and the eastern part was rebuilt. This is the northwest tower and the western end of the nave. (The lower part of the tower is Norman — the upper part was blown down in 1210 and replaced in the style of the time — 'Early English'.) Notice the round-headed windows and doors, the flat buttresses, the Norman clerestory windows and the frilly corbel table. The aisle windows are also Early English.

Norman Parish Churches

Involved as they were in their great programme of building castles and rebuilding Saxon cathedrals and monastic churches, the Normans largely neglected parish churches until the 12th century. Some of the larger landowners built new simple stone parish churches before that, but the bulk of Norman parish churches date from c1130 onwards.

Early Norman churches are usually quite primitive and as they were often built by Saxon workers, many have Saxon characteristics and there is a period of transition between the two styles. Later Norman churches have similar characteristics to their cathedrals and abbey churches and like those buildings, those that survive tend to have been extensively rebuilt and embellished in later centuries as the population grew. It was during the Norman era that many of our existing parishes became established and there is thus a substantial number of churches in England, Wales and Lowland Scotland with Norman origins. (As with **Norman Cathedrals**, those listed below are those that have remained predominantly Norman although traces of Norman styles and work are to be found in a vast number of other churches up and down the country.) Their main characteristics are listed below.

Above:
St Michael, Duntisbourne Rouse, Gloucestershire. A simple Cotswold church that has a Saxon nave and an early Norman chancel. As all these parish churches were probably built by Saxon workers, the presence of Saxon features like long and short work may not be significant for dating. Here the big window is 15th century and the upper part of the tower is dated 1587.

Left:
St Michael, Stewkley, Buckinghamshire. An unaltered Norman village church of c1150; note blind arcading on the tower, round-headed door and window openings, and zig-zag design round the windows. Notice the three arches of the west doorway, two blanked, and the unusually shaped tympanum over the main door.

Plan: Before c1130, rectangular with a short nave, without aisles, and with a small asped chancel. Little decoration. After c1130, longer aisled naves, and square ended chancels, west bell towers become more frequent. (Exceptions are the round churches of the Knights Templar, which are copies of Jerusalem churches seen during the crusades.)

Elevation and Walling: Tall and thick, mostly rubble, some ashlar. Aisle arcading has heavy drum piers, and plain round arches in the early Norman period, piers with composite columns, and multi-order arches in the late Norman.

Doors and Windows: Doors are small with a decorated tympanum in the early Norman period, multi-order arches highly decorated later (see below). Windows are tall, narrow and round headed.

Carving and Decoration: Very little until c1130, thereafter progressively more elaborate. Circa 1130 chevron carving, capitals sculpted with foliage and scroll designs. Circa 1140 beakhead and animal carvings. Circa 1150 increased use of carvings of human figures. Circa 1160 highly ornamental multi-order arches, decorated corbel heads. Circa 1180 stained glass begins to appear.

Locations

Scotland:

Birnie, Grampian, early Norman church, c1120-50; **Leuchars**, Fife, Romanesque, c1190; **Dalmeny**, Lothian, Romanesque, c1150-60; **St Andrews**, Fife, church of St Rule's, c1140, with earlier tower.

Wales:

Margam, West Glamorgan, former late Norman abbey church but simple, c1150; **St Clear's**, Dyfed, early Norman, c1110-20.

Below:

St Mary, Iffley, Oxon. A late Norman church (c1175) and the gift of a rich patron, Iffley is elaborately decorated. All the usual Romanesque features are here although the church has been restored several times over the centuries. The rose window with its zig-zag mouldings, for example, is Victorian.

England:

North — **St Bees**, Cumbria, former nunnery church, late Norman, c1160; **Old Beswick**, Northumberland, early Norman, c1120; **Weaverthorpe**, North Humberside, early Norman, c1110; **Prestbury**, Cheshire, small late Norman church in grounds of later parish church, c1160.

Midlands — **Sempringham**, Lincolnshire, late Norman, c1160; **Kilpeck**, Hereford, outstanding late Norman church, c1140-50; **Elkstone**, Gloucestershire, important late Norman, c1170; **Iffley**, Oxford, major late Norman church, c1170.

East Anglia — **Holy Sepulchre**, Cambridgeshire, circular nave, 'Templar' style church, c1130; **Polstead**, Suffolk, Norman *brick* church, c1180-1200.

Southeast — **Chobham**, Surrey, late Norman arcade and chapel, c1180, early Norman nave; **Pyrford**, Surrey, early Norman, c1100; **Barfreston**, Kent, late Norman, c1190; **New Shoreham**, West Sussex, major Norman church, tower and transepts, c1120, chancel, c1180-90.

Southwest — **Studland**, Dorset, classic early Norman, nave, c1090, parts later, c1120; **Lullington**, Somerset, late Norman, c1150; **Compton Martin**, Somerset, major late Norman church, c1120; **Mortenstow**, Cornwall, late Norman, c1150.

THE GOTHIC ERA, c1200-1630

The Medieval Period, c1200-1530

The period of history known to historians as the Middle Ages coincides with the flowering of one of the great historic architectural styles which we now call the 'Gothic' although by no means all medieval architecture was Gothic nor is all Gothic architecture medieval. Indeed both terms, medieval (or 'Middle Ages') and Gothic, are inventions of later periods. 'Middle Ages' is a largely 19th century concept of the period between the Dark Ages and the Renaissance — about 800AD to 1500 — which from our later perspective we have narrowed down to that from the end of the 12th century to the beginning of the 16th century. The term 'Gothic' derived originally from the French implying of Germanic or Teutonic origin but, after the Renaissance, came to be used, sometimes perjoratively, to describe any architecture or decoration that was not Classical (ie Greek or Roman) in origin — the barbarian Goths, of course, having sacked Rome in 410AD.

The Medieval period is that of the predominance of the Christian religion in men's lives — women being mere chattels — and more particularly of the dominance of the Roman church with its rigid structure of belief, ceremonial and hierarchy. It began with the proliferation of the monasteries throughout Britain and ended with their Dissolution and the onset of the Reformation. It began at a time when almost all knowledge was Latin-based and religious, the province of the monks and the clergy, and ended when much of the ancient world's store of wisdom could be read in English, French or German. It began too, when the ownership of land and feudalism dominated both the church and society at large and came to an end when a prosperous, educated and largely secular and urban middle class began to assert itself. In dynastic terms in England, the Middle Ages begin about the time of the reign of the Angevin king Henry II (1154-89) and end rather more precisely perhaps with that of Henry VIII (1509-47). In Scotland it begins with the Normanised David I and ends with James IV — and Flodden. And throughout this period and for some time afterwards, the prevailing building style was Gothic.

What then is the Gothic style? It is not just, as many believe, simply the substitution of the pointed for the rounded arch, although the pointed arch is

Right:

The spirit of Gothic architecture — the west front of Lincoln Cathedral soars heavenwards and expresses in stone the aspirations of four centuries of English church builders — from Norman to 15th century. The lower level is basically Norman — note the round arches to all the main openings and the depth of the walling — but the whole facade has been extended out beyond the Norman aisles and is 'Early English' in style, c1235, including the turrets. The Early English lancet arcades of the upper levels have gabled niches for figures of saints. The three west windows are all Perpendicular ('perp') in style and were installed in the late 14th century. The twin west towers were heightened late in the 15th century again in the 'perp' style with ogee arches at the top of the bell openings. They originally had needle spires but these were taken down in 1807.

its main indicator, Gothic is an entire art form in itself extending beyond architecture to sculpture, wood-carving, furniture, decoration and stained glass. It is in effect the counter-point to the Classical style and its interplay with that style makes up the main theme of not only British but Western architectural history throughout the ages. By the mid-17th century, Gothic had been almost completely replaced by the Classical as the dominant style in these islands and remained in eclipse for about the next 200 years when, in the Victorian period, it was to flower again as vigorously as ever. Even so, it never entirely died out and several important buildings in the Gothic style appeared in both the 17th and 18th centuries.

The technical advantage of the pointed arch over the semicircular rounded one is that the height of the arch is no longer determined by its width. Arches and consequently roofs could be raised to give a feeling of spaciousness and grace not possible with the more ponderous rounded Romanesque. In an age too, when religious symbolism was paramount, the upward pointing arch — like hands held together in prayer — was of immense significance. Indeed, it

Left:
Castles were the other great creation of the Gothic era. This is the entrance to the inner ward of Caerphilly Castle in Wales, begun c1271. It demonstrates an essential aspect of Gothic architecture: verticality in its elevation — 'if it doesn't have a tower, it can't be Gothic' — and its overwhelming size.

may have been this aspect that led to its adoption in the first place. Scholars differ on the actual date and place of the first use of the pointed arch and the ribbed vault associated with it in western Europe — the earliest in Britain was in Durham cathedral in 1104 — but most agree that its use followed very quickly upon the experience of the First Crusade which was launched in 1095. Of the technical advantages it conferred, there is no such doubt. In essence, the rounded Romanesque arch meant that the downward and outward thrust of the roof had to be carried by the walls and in consequence those walls had to be very thick. When openings were made in the walls — arcades, doorways, etc — their arches had to be supported on massive piers. With the pointed arch and its ribbed vaulting, the thrust from the roof could be directed to the corners of the bays and borne there by piers supported by buttresses, either close-set or of the 'flying' type, leaving the intervening walls largely free from load. Thus, compared with the Romanesque — or Norman — style the Gothic meant:

(1) that thick walls were no longer needed.
(2) that larger windows were possible without affecting structural strength.
(3) piers could also be reduced in weight and thickness.

In short, the arrival of the Gothic style set the master builders free to open up and, literally, to enlighten their churches in a manner quite impossible previously. How this was done in the succeeding centuries is the story of Gothic and the subsidiary styles that developed within the main style. From the 13th century to the 17th century it was virtually the only style for ecclesiastical buildings. More than nine tenths of our village churches built in the period are Gothic, as are most town churches. Every cathedral except those built since the Reformation has Gothic features and there survives a plethora of castles, medieval manor houses, guildhalls and market halls all styled in Gothic. And we should perhaps recall that for much of the Gothic era, England was the architectural leader of the western world.

The change from late-Norman Romanesque to Gothic did not, of course, come in suddenly. There was the usual period of transition and there are numerous examples of buildings dating from the period 1150 to 1190 that have characteristics of both styles. Many of these buildings are the monasteries built by the Cistercian order which began to replace the Benedictine in England towards the end of the 12th century. An austere and, in modern parlance, a more radical order than the Benedictines, the Cistercians eschewed the architectural enrichment of the late Norman style. Although they retained the Romanesque rounded archway and the heavy walling, they also brought in the pointed arch and the ribbed vault and the corbel that supported it. The impressive ruins of Fountains Abbey in North Yorkshire are the outstanding testimony of their work and of the transitional period (see **Medieval Monasteries**). Of the transitional period too are major parts of the cathedrals of Canterbury, Worcester and the abbey church at Glastonbury (see **Gothic Cathedrals**).

The first truly 'Gothic' cathedral in England was Wells in Somerset, completed in 1190 (the celebrated west front was finished in 1229). It had pointed arches, ribbed vaulting and clusters of columns encircling the piers. Its windows were of the pointed, lancet type, a feature of this early form of Gothic known as 'Early English', or 'First Pointed', and the first of the terms describing the phases of Gothic subsidiary styles established in the 19th century by Thomas Rickman (d1841). 'Early English' or 'First Pointed' covers the period 1190 to 1280; the 'dec' from 1280 to 1350; and the 'perp' from 1350 to 1510. Once again, these dates are only general indicators of the progress of an evolving style whose emergence in reality probably depended upon the chance arrival in an area of a particular master mason or sculptor for the Gothic style is highly individualistic. Inevitably, too, there are variations in date from area to area. In the Middle Ages, just as ideas tended to flow northwards across western Europe from Italy to France, Germany and eventually to Britain, so within Britain, ideas tended to spread from south to north and rather more slowly from east to west. These divisions of the Gothic have other limitations in the interpretation of style but they are now in general use and we shall use them to examine, in later pages, our great heritage of Medieval Gothic buildings.

Apart from the great cathedrals and castles and a few stone built palaces and manor houses, the bulk of building in the Middle Ages was in timber — brick did not begin to come into use until the late 13th century. Of these buildings — timber-framed with wattle and daub infilling under a thatched or shingled roof — virtually none survive from the 13th century, a handful from the 14th century, more from the 15th century and the 16th century. Since timbers tended to be used over and over again, and, kept dry, old oak is virtually indestructible, some timbers from the early Middle Ages are no doubt still in place in buildings of a later date. But these buildings owe nothing to either the Romanesque or the Gothic styles of architecture. Their origins are in the Saxon open hall tradition and from them evolved what is perhaps the most distinctive domestic and vernacular architectural style to be found in these islands (see **The Timber-Framed Tradition**).

Gothic Cathedrals and Churches

EARLY ENGLISH c1190-1290

Known nowadays as 'Early English', the first wholly Gothic style to be introduced into Britain spread to church buildings large and small from three main sources — the choirs of Canterbury Cathedral built c1174 in the southeast, Wells Cathedral in the west and Rievaulx Abbey in the north. The main characteristics of this style are listed below.

Plan: Buildings became more rectangular and were extended eastwards, with square ends (apses disappeared) — choirs in the case of abbey churches and cathedrals, chancels in the case of parish churches. Churches were enlarged by the addition of aisles or by building new naves to use the earlier ones as aisles.

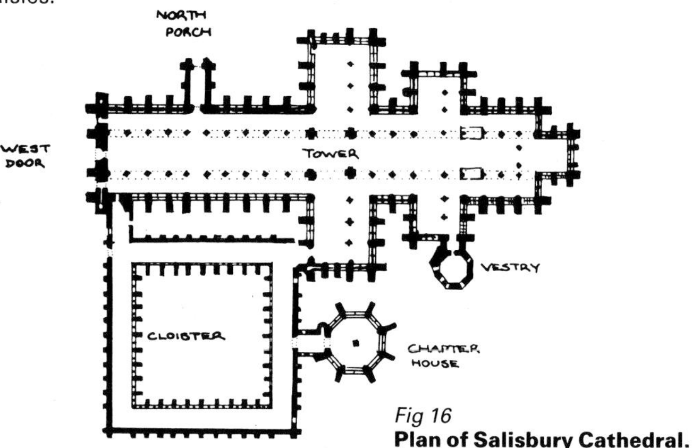

Fig 16
Plan of Salisbury Cathedral.

Elevation and Walling: The pointed arch completely replaced the rounded one. Ridge vaulting and the use of buttresses allowed thinner walls, smaller piers and bigger windows. Vaulting steadily became more elaborate; the tierceron vault was introduced in Lincoln in 1240. The use of Purbeck marble at Canterbury and Lincoln set a fashion for detached shafts. West fronts in the form of massive screens of niched figures (as at Wells) are an EE feature.

Roofing: Tended to be high pitched like thatched or tiled roofs but lead covered. Pitch was reduced later to avoid lead creep but traces of earlier roofs are sometimes visible on the walling of towers.

Windows: Windows increased in size and area both to give more light and increasingly to display stained glass. Basic window shapes employed tall lancets without mullions, grouped in threes or fives within a pointed arch. Drip moulds surround the arches. Window tracery developed throughout the period, see below.

Window Tracery: One of the real guides to identifying Gothic periods, window tracery takes two main forms:

Fig 17
Gothic window tracery: 1 Plate tracery; 2 Bar tracery (geometric); 3 Decorated ('dec'); 4 Perpendicular ('perp').

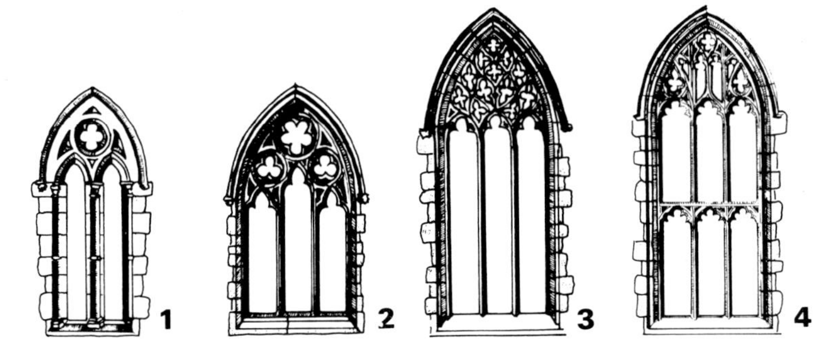

Plate Tracery when the flat stones between the tips of the lancets in a window were perforated by simple designs in the form of circles, later trefoils or quatrefoils. These areas of stone between lancets were gradually reduced in thickness and became mullions and brought in.
Bar Tracery in which the mullions continue up into the window head to form a decorative mesh or pattern. The tracery of the late Early English period (from c1250) is known as 'Geometric' and comprises mainly circles or foiled (ie cusped in section) circles.

Above:
Salisbury Cathedral, Wiltshire. Built as a single unit and not piecemeal over the centuries like others, Salisbury was constructed in 1220-80 and epitomises the 'Early English' style. Notice: 1 The tall lancet windows in groups of twos and threes; 2 The deep angle buttresses taking the outward thrust of the roof vaulting of the aisles; 3 The flying buttresses carrying the same thrust of the main roof over the aisles. Walls are thinner, windows are bigger, buttresses deeper than in Norman times.

Left:
Down Ampney Church, Gloucestershire, at the other end of the scale, Early English lancet windows in a village church consecrated in 1265 and 'restored' in 1863. Note the arcading on the tower and the flat buttresses.

Decoration and Ornament: Multiple columns with detached shafts in Purbeck marble or polished limestone; capitals carved with characteristic deeply under cut 'stiff-leaf' motif, deep mouldings, and 'dogtooth' carving; piscina are now found in many churches.

Locations

Many large churches and cathedrals have features of all the varied Gothic styles as extension and rebuilding continued throughout the period. A summary of the major examples is shown in the table at the end of this section. Although parish churches with Early English features are to be found throughout the country many have, like the cathedrals and abbey churches, also been subject to later building in more advanced styles.

DECORATED, c1290-1350

The term 'Decorated' as applied to the style of Gothic architecture which developed in the late 13th and early 14th centuries, takes its name primarily from the richness and variety of the window tracery that then came into vogue. In summary, it can be described as 'more tracery than glass'.

Bar tracery gradually replaced plate tracery and at first, until about 1315, usually assumed 'geometrical' shapes in the window heads — 'Y', or intersecting, tracery or of simple and barbed circles. Then, as one authority has suggested, masons began experimenting with their compasses and went on to introduce a variety of 'curvilinear' shapes. At the same time, the 'ogee' (ie double 'S') arch made its appearance from the Continent and was adopted with almost gay abandon in England. The use of free-flowing tracery curves — 'daggers', tongues of flame, the interlace of branches in a woodland glade are all analogies used — also spread to walling and to vaulting. By the middle of the 14th century, this form of 'middle-pointed' Gothic had degenerated to a writhing style in France known as 'flamboyant' but in England, it gave way to a more restrained Gothic style, the 'rectilinear' or the 'Perpendicular'. Again, however, the division is not clear cut. The two styles continued to intermingle for a long period. Among major influences was the devastating effect of the Black Death which between 1348 and 1351 killed off a quarter of

Above:

Tewkesbury Abbey, Gloucestershire. The cluster of chapels around the east end of Tewkesbury Abbey shows the evolution of window tracery: 1 Stepped lancets are early 'dec'; 2 Cusped tracery at the end of the lancets; 3 The choir windows display the sinuous tracery of later 'dec' enriched by ballflower and crowned by gables. Note also the pierced battlements and the flying buttresses.

Below:

The east end of Chichester Cathedral rebuilt after the fire of 1187. Note: 1 The Early English lancets; 2 The rose window, in style c1280 but renewed; 3 The windows of the Lady Chapel built c1290-1300 with their varieties of 'dec' tracery.

the population, hitting priests, monks and their lay helpers including many craftsmen particularly hard. One of the effects of this decimation of skills coupled with the growing economic effects of the wool trade was a shift in emphasis away from the more monumental church buildings under the auspices of the monasteries, towards the building of parish churches. Modern scholars, however, tend to refute earlier suggestions that the effects of the Black Death hastened the introduction of the Perpendicular style, pointing out that the style existed alongside the Decorated long before the plague struck.

The first examples of 'Decorated' are to be found in Westminster Abbey (after 1245) and at Exeter Cathedral (after c1280). The main characteristics of the style are listed below.

Plan: The introduction of polygonal shapes instead of squared ones so that windows could be shown at oblique angles in chapels and chapter houses.

Elevation and Walling: Walls were divided into 12-15ft (3.7-4.6m) bays between buttresses, with receding set-offs as buttresses rose either to the parapet or to a pinnacle. Parapets have wide gutters behind them with rain-spouts, some gargoyled, at intervals. Early on a simple coping on the parapet but an increasing use of battlements came later in the period.

Vaulting: Increasing elaboration of vaulting — pattern — 'star' vaults and 'net' vaults (curvilinear, like window tracery), elaborate decoration of ribs and bosses. Piers and columns tall and slender, and formed into clusters.

Roofing: Low pitch timber roofs covered with lead. Internally much artistic carpentry in roof timbering, hammer beams, decorative panelling.

Bell-towers: A general proliferation of bell towers at the west end of naves, with arches between. Buttressed at corners — angle buttresses early, diagonal or set-back later. The west door was largely used for processional purposes; the main frontispiece and entrance to the church became the south door.

Windows: Pointed or ogee shaped window arches surrounded by shaped drip mould with carved stops. Lancet windows with thick stone mullions and plate tracery at the head give way to thin mullions ending in complicated, often fantastic, free curvilinear shapes at the window head — moulded, cusped and barbed. There was much greater use of stained glass depicting saints and biblical scenes, etc.

Fig 18
Capitals compared: 1 Norman; 2 Early English; 3 Decorated.

Above left:
Chapter House, Southwell, Nottinghamshire. Here trefoiled plate tracery, the pierced parapet and the pinnacles c1300 mark the transition from Early English to 'dec'.

Above right:
'Dec' into 'perp' c1360 — the west front of SS Mary, Katherine & All Saints, Edington, Wiltshire. The aisle windows are 'dec', the eight-light window above is 'perp'. Note the double portal.

Spires: Timber broaches give way to needle spires within parapets with corner buttresses, pinnacles, etc.

Decoration: Apart from windows and capitals, the elaborate decoration of tombs and monuments in some places almost gets out of hand — stone foliage of tropical lushness and complexity. Wood carving also added to the over-decoration of church interiors — pew ends, misericords, and most especially in the screens between nave and chancel or choir and reredos behind altars.

PERPENDICULAR, 1335-1530

The style of architecture known as Rectilinear or Perpendicular is representative of the long final flowering of the 'High Gothic' in Britain and covers a period of about 200 years. It is essentially an English style and it is not to be found outside the United Kingdom except in a few places where the English built churches, like Ireland and Calais. As with the Decorated style, the name Perpendicular derives from the pattern of its window tracery which is a development of the panel effects of reticulated tracery where each panel

Above:
The West Window, St George's Chapel, Windsor shows 'perp' in all its glory and dates from 1503-9. Note: 1 15 lancets or lights, four transoms, and a four-centred arch on top and in each of the 80 panels, a saint, a warrior, a bishop or a king in stained glass, and in one of them, perhaps, William Vertue, the chapel's master builder; 2 Three statues above the door are in Coade stone, put in in 1799; 3 Flying buttresses over the aisles and a pinnacle surmounted by a 'King's Beast'.

Right:
St George's Chapel from the South showing seven bays of the chancel with the Lincoln Chapel at the end. Note the deep stepped buttresses topped with pinnacles and 'King's Beasts', the pierced battlements and the four-centre arches to the aisle windows.

is compressed laterally to give it straight sides. In summary we now have 'more glass than tracery'. Slender vertical mullions have regular horizontal divisions to give rows of panels, each panel arched and cusped. This network of vertical and horizontal tracery panels is often applied to walling. The impression is one of a delicate stone cage and the same effect comes from the slender fan vaulting which accompanies it. Although it was used for large structural alterations in a number of cathedrals, Perpendicular is more suited to smaller buildings like chantry chapels and major tombs. It reaches its climax in the three royal chapels of St George's, Windsor (1475-1528); King's College, Cambridge (1508-15) and Henry VII's chapel in Westminster Abbey (1503-19). But perhaps its greatest contribution to English church architecture lies in the splendid legacy of the great 'wool' churches of the Cotswolds, East Anglia and South Yorkshire, and a plethora of 'perpendicular' towers elsewhere, all built by secular and private wealth. In the 16th century, the Perpendicular began slowly to merge with Renaissance classical motifs and to become what we now call 'Tudor' or 'Elizabethan'.

Plan: Rebuilt churches become large open aisled halls with slender moulded columns with a proliferation of chantry chapels and an enlargement of south porches, some multi-storied.

Elevation and Walling: Large windows tend to fill the entire wall space between deep stepped buttresses which terminate in crocketed pinnacles. Fine ashlar masonry gives a clean bare look. Parapets are invariably battlemented sometimes in miniature and often with pierced tracery or strapwork.

Roofing: Many churches were re-roofed to add a clerestory with high, large windows. Elaborately carved or painted internal roof timbering is a major feature.

Above left:
South Porch, St John the Baptist, Cirencester, Gloucestershire. Built about 1490 by the local abbey, probably for secular purposes, and after the Dissolution used a town hall, this imposing building demonstrates the 'perp' in a domestic setting — note the canted oriel windows and the elaborate buttresses with niches.

Above right:
Elegant towers on 'wool' churches are one of the glories of the 'perp' period. Here is one of them: Huish Episcopi, Somerset (c1505).

Windows: Window arches begin to become lower — less pointed — later in the period with much use of the four-centre and the Tudor arches often within squared off hood or bracket moulds with decorated stops. Spandrels are carved with geometric designs.

Towers: Perpendicular west towers were added to many churches as well as cathedrals. Tall, with diagonal, set-back or clasping buttresses, tall tracery panels, battlemented parapets, with tracery or pierced, corner pinnacles, high and crocketed. Long narrow belfry openings, sometimes with pierced stone screens. Stair turrets are a feature in some parts.

Spires: Parapeted, battlemented and pinnacled spires with gabled window openings. Some flying buttresses are a feature and many stone lanterns date from the Perpendicular period.

Chantry Chapels and Tombs: Elaborate chantry chapels like stonework cages and highly decorated tombs — later ones reflecting Renaissance motifs — are a distinctive feature of the late Perpendicular style.

British cathedral buildings styles

Cathedral	*Nave*	*Choir*	*Transepts*	*Crypt*	*Notes*
Bath Abbey	Perp	Perp	Perp	—	Rebuilt 1500-39
Carlisle	Dec	EE/Dec	Perp	—	Superb Dec east window
Canterbury	Perp	Dec	Norman	Norman	—
Chester	Perp/Dec	Dec/EE	Dec	—	Extended south transept
Chichester	Norm/EE	Norm/Trans	Norm/Trans	—	Lady Chapel Dec
Durham	Norman	Norm/EE	Norman	—	Choir transept EE
Ely	Norman	EE	Norman	—	Lady Chapel Dec
Exeter	Dec	Dec	Norman towers	—	Perp west front
Glasgow	Dec	Dec	Dec	—	Vaulted undercroft
Gloucester	Norman	Norm/Perp	Norman	Norman	Lady Chapel Perp
Lichfield	EE	Dec	EE	—	EE Chapter House
Lincoln	EE	EE	EE	—	Norman west front
Llandaff	EE/Dec	Dec	Dec	—	Much restored in recent times
Norwich	Norman	Norm/EE	Norman	—	Cloister; Perp transept screen
Oxford	Norm/Perp	Norm/EE/Dec	Norman	—	Latin Chapel mainly Dec
Ripon	Perp	Trans/Dec	Trans	Saxon	EE west front
Salisbury	EE	EE	EE	—	Dec Chapter House and Cloister
Southwick	Modern	EE	Perp/EE	—	—
Southwell	Norman	EE	Norman	—	Dec Chapter House
St Albans	Norman	Norm/Perp	Norman	—	EE west front
St Davids	Norm/Dec	Norm/Dec	Norm/EE	—	—
Wells	EE	EE	EE	—	Dec Lady Chapel & Chapter House
Winchester	Perp	EE	Norman	Norman	—
Worcester	Norm/Trans	EE	Norman	Norman	Norm & Perp Chapter House
York	Dec	Perp	EE	Norman	Dec Chapter House

Medieval Castles

The strongly fortified castle continued to exercise a dominant role both in military affairs and in the social order throughout the Middle Ages. It played a key role in protecting the Welsh and Scottish border areas from marauders in both directions, in the subjection of Wales and in countering the threat of a French invasion of southern England in the late 14th century. Its role in the maintenance of internal law and order was, however, even more significant. When royal authority was strong, the king controlled the building of castles and used his own castles to keep a watch on possible dissidents. Under weaker kings like Henry VI (1422-61), royal castles were neglected, and private castles in the hands of what were known as 'bastard-feudal' lords and their bands of mercenaries held sway over the countryside.

But, as ever, the march of military technology was never halted. Siege weapons were steadily improved in both hitting power and range even before the arrival of gunpowder and cannon and the design of new or existing castles had to be improved to counter them. The curtain wall castle of the late Norman era like that at Framlingham became the norm. Vulnerable rectangular wall towers were replaced by sapper-proof octagonal, round or 'D-shaped' towers with immensely thick batters, each tower becoming in effect, a keep in its own right. (Quite often massive Norman keeps were incorporated as wall forts.) Entrance gates — always a weak point — were highly fortified with double 'drum' towers, portcullises, machicolations, 'murder-holes' and drawbridges. Greater use was made of water defences, not just moats but extensive lakes or inundations as at Kenilworth where they covered over 100 acres. The ultimate medieval castle was concentric — ward within fortified ward and surrounded by water. But by the time of the Wars of the Roses (another Victorian title) from 1455-85, cannon were already making medieval castles obsolete and it became now the case that he who controlled the gunpowder and the cannon controlled the land. Cannon, it is said, made Warwick the kingmaker. And the kings he made — the Tudors — made certain that they ever after kept a tight control on powder, tube and shot.

But the arrival of the cannon was only one factor in the demise of the medieval castle. After the Black Death had decimated the population, the high cost of labour and materials made the building of castles capable of withstanding sophisticated siege prohibitively expensive even for kings. Nor were they necessary when the main threat came from bands of marauders rather than from organised armies. At the same time, priorities were changing. Domestic comfort and culture gained in importance in the lives of the land-owners, lordlings and bishops alike. Aristocratic status continued to demand that the lord should live in his castle and the royal licence to crenellate remained a valued symbol of standing and loyalty. So, the fortified manor house — still perhaps even called a castle and looking very much like one — began to take the place of the ancient 'donjohn'. And where lords still lived in genuine castles, they spent more on the improvement of their halls and their kitchens than they did on their portcullises and barbicans. The castle was not, however, completely dead. It reappears in Tudor, Georgian and Victorian times in the guise of the fort and the fort did not finally expire until 1940 and the arrival of air power.

Scotland has a legacy of medieval castles but they are different in style from those of England and Wales. Edward I (1272-1307) never succeeded in holding down Scotland with chains of impregnable stone castles as he had done in Wales. Largely because of lack of money, he built only in timber. The only castles in the English concentric style are to be found in the Borders — Tantallon is one example. Most Scottish castles were built by powerful lairds and follow the fashion of the pele or tower house. These were, by the late Middle Ages, tall, very strong keeps — almost solid masses of stone masonry honeycombed with rooms, passages and stairs. Each storey had a vaulted roof and was virtually fire-proof.

Plan: The Norman-style keep is replaced by a rectangular or polygonal inner curtain wall with regularly spaced drum towers or 'enceinte' enclosing the inner ward or bailey which contains the lord's private accommodation — his

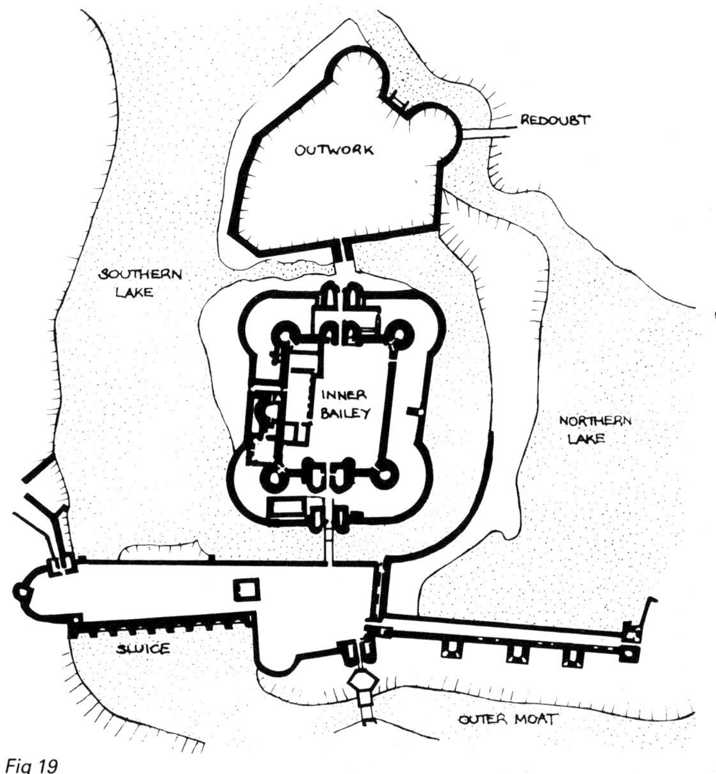

Fig 19
Plan of Caerphilly Castle, Wales.

Above:
Caerphilly Castle, South Glamorgan. The most advanced and elaborate castle in Britain when it was built between 1268-77, Caerphilly has formidable water defences and awesome fortifications. The central stronghold is double-ringed and in part triple-ringed — one of the first of the new concentric designs to be built. It was carefully restored in the 19th century. 1 Outer defensive dam and wall; 2 South lake running into inner moat; 3 Walls of middle ward with towers and sally ports; 4 Walls of inner ward; 5 Inner ward tower; 6 West gatehouses on both walls; 7 East gatehouses; 8 Leaning inner ward tower, slighted with gunpowder in the Civil War.

Below:
The south gateway at Caerphilly, a barbican guarding access to the outer dam leading to the main east gateways.

Right:
Said to be the most fought over castle in Britain, Kidwelly Castle, Dyfed, was founded by the Normans but rebuilt c1291 in its present concentric form for Edward I probably by James of St George who built many of the English castles in Wales. This is its main gatehouse completed in 1422 with drawbridge, portcullis, gates on the outside and inside with a vault full of arrow slits and 'murder-holes' — slots to drop missiles through — in between.

Above:
Bodiam Castle, East Sussex. Licence to crenellate was given to the owner of Bodiam in 1386 but it is more of a fortified manor house than a fighting castle. Compare it with Caerphilly.

hall, his solar, his kitchen, private chapel, etc. An outer defensive curtain wall with towers surrounds the inner ward and contains an outer ward which houses the garrison. In some castles there is a third defensive wall covering a middle ward. Outer gatehouses are now very strong and fitted with the latest military technology with a portcullis and drawbridge, etc, all within a wide deep moat or other water obstacle. A barbican — a fortified outer entrance stands on an island or on the far side of the moat. Outer and inner gateways are offset.

Elevation and Walling: Inner walling is thick enough to contain accommodation in the upper storeys, each tower is a keep in itself with access only from the courtyard or from a rampart walk on top of the walls.

Outer curtain walling 7ft (2m) thick, 35ft (5.5m) high with a rampart walk between towers. Walls and towers all battlemented, some towers, especially gatehouses, have machicolations. Built of heavy masonry blocks and usually ashlared. Some castles were whitewashed.

Windows: Small lancet type crossbow slits on the outside walls. Larger windows inside the inner bailey in domestic buildings and often adopting Gothic styles in window tracery, notably in chapels.

Left:
Scottish castles were different. Here are two of them: Caerlaverock Castle, D&G, an English castle built c1290 and taken by the Scots — the ruined house was built in the 1630s; Hermitage Castle, Borders, built 1296 and restored in the 19th century. It was owned by Lord Soulis, Scotland's 'Dracula'. *All John Mackay*

Below:
Walmer Castle, Kent. Built as one of three similar forts by Henry VIII c1540 to guard The Downs anchorage, Walmer has the typical post-gunpowder low profile, a deep circular moat, a four-lobed keep with massive gun-ports and a circular central redoubt. The obviously domestic buildings are later, c1720, now the home of the Lord Warden of the Cinque Ports. The tower is Victorian.

TUDOR CASTLES

The development of effective artillery meant that by the Tudor era, the national legacy of medieval castles had largely been deprived of its military significance and those owning castles concentrated on converting them into more comfortable modern homes. But the role of the fort — a type of castle designed to withstand bombardment whilst itself possessing substantial firepower — was by no means over. Henry VIII was, among other things, an expert on artillery. In 1538 when he perceived a threatened invasion from the Continent following his excommunication by the Pope, he quickly strengthened his coastal defences by building a string of forts from the Thames estuary round to the mouth of the Fal. He also strengthened the

Fig 20
A Tudor castle. Plan of Walmer.

defences of Harwich, Hull and Holy Island. Although there is some suggestion that he may have designed some of the forts himself, an early prototype of the more modern arrangements already existed at Dartmouth. Built to resist Henry Tudor in 1481, its design may have come from ideas seen in Europe, notably from an Italian, Sammichele, at Verona. Later in the 16th century, Elizabeth had the defences of Berwick modernised in similar style.

Locations

Scotland:

ENGLISH STYLE: **Bothwell**, Strathclyde, 13th century (SSS); **Caerlaverock**, D&G, c1290 (SSS); **Tantallon**, Lothian, 14th century (SSS).

SCOTTISH STYLE: **Hermitage**, Borders, 1450 (SSS); **Neidpath**, Borders, 1250.

Wales:

Beaumaris, Anglesey, c1300 (Cadw); **Caernarvon**, Gwynedd, 1285-1322 (Cadw); **Caerphilly**, Mid-Glamorgan, c1270-1300 (Cadw); **Chepstow**, Gwent, 13th century (Cadw); **Chirk**, Clwyd, c1310 (NT); **Denbigh**, Clwyd, c1282 (Cadw); **Harlech**, Gwynedd, 1283-90 (Cadw); **Kidwelly**, Dyfed, c1275-1325 (Cadw); **Manorbier**, Dyfed, 13th century; **Raglan**, Gwent, 15th century (Cadw); **Rhuddlan**, Clwyd, c1277-82 (Cadw).

England:

North — **Alnwick**, Northumberland, 14th century; **Dunstanburgh**, Northumberland, 14th century (EH); **Raby**, Durham, 14th century; **Warkworth**, Northumberland, 15th century (EH); **Bolton**, North Yorkshire, 14th century.

TUDOR: **Berwick on Tweed**, Northumberland, town walls, c1558; **Lindisfarne Castle**, 1550 (NT).

Midlands — **Goodrich**, Herefordshire and Worcestershire, 13th century (EH); **Kenilworth**, Warwickshire, 14th century (EH); **Ludlow**, Salop, 14th century; **Warwick**, 14th century; **Broughton**, Oxfordshire, 14th century.

East Anglia — **Castle Acre**, Norfolk, 1250 (EH); **Wingfield Castle**, Suffolk, 1350; **Castle Hedingham**, Essex, 12th century.

Southeast — **Donnington**, Berkshire, 14th century; **Windsor**, Berkshire, 14th/15th century; **Bodiam**, East Sussex, 14th century (NT); **Hever**, Kent, 15th century; **Leeds Castle**, Kent, 14th century; **Herstmonceux**, East Sussex, 15th century.

TUDOR: **Yarmouth Castle**, Isle of Wight, 1547 (EH); **Hurst Castle**, Hampshire, 1544 (EH); **Deal Castle**, Kent, 1540 (EH); **Walmer Castle**, Kent, 1593 (EH); **Upnor Castle**, Kent, 1559 (EH).

Southwest — **Corfe Castle**, Dorset, 14th century (NT).

TUDOR: **Pendennis Castle**, Cornwall, 1546 (EH); **St Mawes Castle**, Cornwall, 1550 (EH); **Dartmouth Castle**, Devon, 1481 (EH); **Portland Castle**, Dorset, 1550.

Medieval Monasteries

Monastic establishments of all kinds proliferated throughout Britain during the Middle Ages and monastic ruins are to be found in almost every county. As major landowners, the monasteries became extremely wealthy as the wool trade gradually burgeoned throughout the period — in the 14th century, for example, the abbot of St Edmundsbury was the greatest landowner in Suffolk. Much of this wealth was devoted to the building and rebuilding of abbeys and churches to keep pace with the changing styles of architecture and to give at least the officers of the monasteries a standard of living commensurate with their wealth and status. Besides their monasteries, many abbots also had manorial establishments (often known as granges) to which they would retreat on occasions. Indeed, it was the very lavishness of the life-style and possessions of the monasteries that was to arouse public antipathy, royal greed and their eventual dissolution in the late 1530s.

The first monasteries to be established in Britain in Saxon times were the Celtic orders in Scotland, Ireland and the north of England and the Benedictines in the south. Founded in the 6th century, the Benedictines were sworn to chastity, poverty and obedience but their very prosperity as major landowners in the richer agricultural areas made them grow lax and dissolute, their abbots aspiring to pride and status. Thus by the end of the 11th century, rival and reforming orders began to appear, the largest being the Cistercians taking their name from Citeaux in Burgundy. The Cistercians sought out what we would nowadays call 'greenfield' sites, the wilder places well away from the thriving towns and villages of the southeast. (There were 75 Cistercian houses in England as well as in Scotland — among those surviving as ruins are Fountains, Jervaulx and Kirkstall in Yorkshire, Furness in Lancashire, Calder in Cumbria.) The other monastic orders were all very much smaller: the Cluniacs, the hermit-like Carthusians, the various orders of Canons of which the Augustinians were the biggest, the Premonstratensians and the Gilbertines. In the 14th century these older monastic orders in their self-centred, self-contained world began to lose influence to orders of preaching friars who not only took an enlightened form of Christian message to the people, but also set up educational establishments like Winchester College and New College, Oxford. The Dominicans or Black Friars were the first, followed by the Franciscans, Grey Friars and the Carmelites, the White Friars.

Medieval monastic building tended to follow a set pattern based on the famous abbey of St Gall in Switzerland which was built in the 9th century, and making only local variations to suit the topography and the location of important facilities like the water supply. In the basic lay-out, the church was the focal point of the complex and was usually cruciform in shape with a long nave and choir. The cloister was on the south side of the nave, forming a square with a lawn in the centre. The main domestic buildings were then arranged around the cloister with the dormitory on the west side with direct access into the church. Close to the dormitory was the chapter house — the monastery conference room — and inevitably, the necessarium or

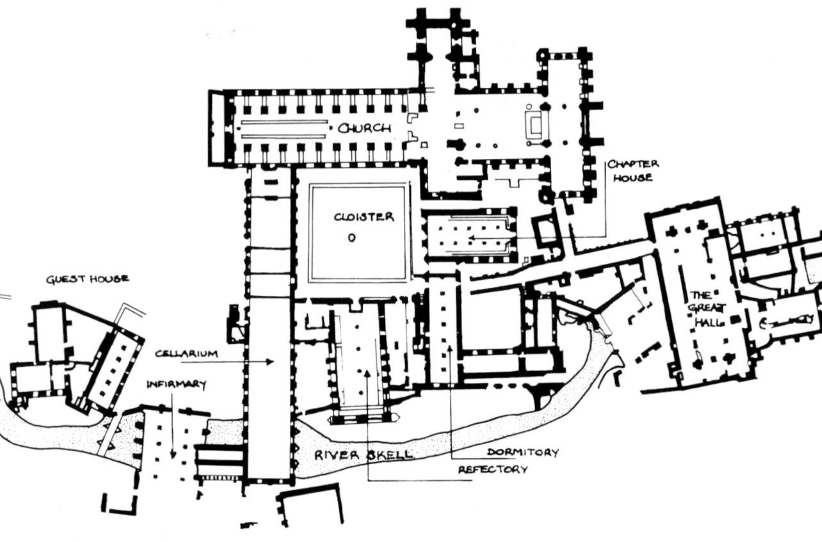

Fig 21
Plan of Fountains Abbey, Yorkshire. Most medieval abbeys follow a similar pattern.

Below:
Fountains Abbey, North Yorkshire. Most of this massive Cistercian Abbey was built between 1148 and 1179 and stands astride the River Skell which provided both waterworks and drainage. 1 The abbey church is a mixture of Romanesque and some of the earliest Gothic in England. The north tower was built c1485 and is largely 'perp'; 2 The Chapter House; 3 The dormitory; 4 The prison block; 5 Novices' day room; 6 Chapel of the Nine Altars (1203-47).

Above:
Talley Abbey, Dyfed. A Premonstratensian abbey built c1200 but much cruder and simpler than the Cistercian houses of the same date.

Right:
Arbroath Abbey, Tayside. Founded by Scotland's William the Lion in 1178, Arbroath Abbey is a rugged example of the Scottish Gothic — simple and bold window proportions, massive buttressed towers. The 'O' window is said to have been used as a beacon for ships.

Above:
Hailes Abbey, Gloucestershire. This row of ruined arches tells something of the story of this Cistercian abbey which was founded in 1246 — a rounded arch on the right, a rounded arch converted into a four-centre one next, then three pointed arches, finally on the left, an ogee arch.

reredorter, the monastic latrine, built over a stream or a water-filled drain. The south side of the cloister was bounded by the refectory — the dining hall — with the kitchen usually close to it, sometimes in a separate building. On the south side too would be the calefactorium or warming room, the only place other than the kitchen where a fire was allowed. In this area would also be located other catering facilities like the bakehouse, the brewhouse and the granary, the stables and the pigsties. On the east side of the cloister would be the cellarium where the produce of the monastic estates was stored usually in a vaulted undercroft. On the east too would be the infirmary not infrequently overlooking the monks' cemetery, and possessing its own small chapel. In the bigger monasteries it was quite usual to find a separate guest house on the site as well as one for the abbot's exclusive use.

Medieval monastic building was invariably in stone and in the Gothic style of architecture of which monastic master-masons — the architects of the day — were supreme practitioners, supported by a wealth of technical skills among the monks and lay brothers of the monastery — stone-masons, sculptors, carvers and carpenters with centuries of tradition behind them. In England and Wales, all such building came to an end 'at a stroke' with the passing of the first Act of Suppression in 1536 under Henry VIII — usually known as the Dissolution. Some monasteries were abandoned and demolished, some became private houses or colleges, others had their churches transferred to the local community — many of our better known cathedrals were originally abbey churches — and their remaining buildings taken down and used as convenient stone quarries. The majority of the former monastic establishments, especially those in country locations have stood in ruins since the 16th century and their attraction to the enthusiast for old buildings is that in their surviving stones, sculpture, moulding and tracery they have preserved a storehouse of the Gothic style free from the embellishments of later generations being, in effect, time capsules of a rich and elaborate architectural style developed at a time when the majority of the people lived in primitive and insanitary hovels.

The following is a list of some of the major abbey ruins to be found in the United Kingdom. The date given is that of the first building in Gothic style — many were founded much earlier and almost all had some rebuilding in the 13th and 14th centuries.

British Abbey Ruins

Abbey	*Approximate Date*	*Order*	*Main styles*
Scotland			
Melrose, Borders*	1136	Cistercian	Decorated
Jedburgh, Borders*	1118	Augustinian	Norman and Transitional
Sweetheart, D&G*	1273	Cistercian	Decorated
Dundrennan, D&G*	1142	Cistercian	Late Norman and Transitional
Kelso, Borders	1128	Benedictine	Late Norman and Transitional
Dryburgh, Borders*	1152	Premonstrat	Norman and Transitional
Coldingham, Borders	1098	Benedictine	Norman
*All SSS			
Wales			
Llanthony, Gwent	1108	Augustinian	Late Norman and Transitional
Ewenny, Mid-Glamorgan	1141	Benedictine	Norman
StrataFlorida, Dyfed*	1201	Cistercian	Late Norman
Talley, Dyfed*	1189	Premonstrat	Early English
Valle Crucis, Clwyd*	1189	Cistercian	Early English
St Dogmaels, Dyfed	1115	Tiron	Norman
Tintern, Gwent*	1131	Cistercian	Decorated
Cymer, Gwynedd*	1199	Cistercian	Early English
*All Cadw			
England — North			
Brinkburn, Northumbria*	1130	Augustinian	Norman
Lindisfarne, Northumbria*	1100	Benedictine	Norman
Fountains, North Yorkshire*	1132	Cistercian	Norman and Transitional
Rievaulx, North Yorkshire	1131	Cistercian	Norman, Transitional, Early English
Guisborough, Cleveland*	1120	Augustinian	Late Norman, Transitional
Whitby, North Yorkshire*	1067	Benedictine	Early English
Furness, Lancashire*	1123	Cistercian	Norman, Decorated and Perpendicular
Midlands			
Crowland, Lincolnshire	1146	Benedictine	Early English
Thornton, South Humberside*	1139	Augustinian	Early Perpendicular
Roche, South Yorkshire*	1170	Cistercian	Early English
Haughmond, Salop*	1135	Augustinian	Norman, Early English
Buildwas, Salop*	1135	Cistercian	Early English, Perpendicular
East Anglia			
Castle Acre, Norfolk*	1090	Cluniac	Late Norman, Early English, Decorated
Walsingham, Norfolk	1150	Augustinian	Early English
Southeast			
Netley, Hants*	1239	Cistercian	Early English, Decorated
Battle, East Sussex*	1076	Benedictine	Early Norman, Decorated
Southwest			
Glastonbury, Somerset	1184	Benedictine	Late Norman
Cleeve, Somerset*	1150	Cistercian	Norman and Early English
*All EH			

Medieval Houses

As we have seen, in Norman times and in the early Middle Ages, the great landowners lived in their castles or their monasteries but they represented only a tiny fraction of the population as a whole. Of the rest, a few local dignitaries like lords of the manor might live in stone houses, a few of which have survived, but wealthy yeomen farmers, rich tradesmen, peasants and labourers all lived in timber or mud houses of which none earlier than the 14th century have come down to us. And it is the houses of the well-to-do that have survived, not the hovels of the poor. Thus when we look at the

Left and below:
The range of medieval houses: The Keep, Tattershall Castle, Lincolnshire. Built by Lord Treasurer Cromwell c1440, Tattershall Castle was still impressively strong — double moat and double bailey and machicolations that worked — but also a grandiose and palatial mansion. Holme Pierrepoint Hall, south range, c1520, four-centred entrance arch flanked by three-storey garde-robe towers.

evolution of British domestic architecture from the Middle Ages onwards, we need to take size and ownership into account. Dr Brunskill in his classic work on vernacular architecture identifies four size-types of houses:

Great houses — The homes of people of national importance, kings and courtiers — castles, palaces.

Large houses ('great' houses in Wales) — The homes of people of local importance, the 'gentry' — manor houses, parsonages, wealthy yeomen farmers, clothiers etc.

Small houses — Houses occupied by ordinary farmers, minor officials, shopkeepers, etc.

Cottages — The homes of labourers and those at subsistence level.

Of these groups, all the 'great' houses and many of the 'large' houses would have been subject to some form of professional design and hence fall into the 'polite' category rather than the vernacular although very often they established a basic style which the locally built vernacular later copied. Throughout the period and beyond it, the old master mason and the carpenter maintained their importance. By the early 16th century, skilled men calling themselves 'architects' and 'surveyors' were appearing, some of them having studied in Italy and bringing back with them the seeds of that great revolution in the arts and architecture we call the Renaissance which was to end the Gothic era. A further sub-division in medieval house building concerns the method of construction and hence the materials used — a division suggested by Lyndon Cave in his book on smaller houses — 'mass construction' where the walls take the strain of the roof, and 'frame' construction where the weight is taken by a timber (or metal) frame. In the former category come all the stone built medieval houses which have survived and an unknown number of cob (baked mud) and similar houses which have not. In the second category are the vast numbers of timber-framed houses that were originally built in the Middle Ages and like all living buildings were enlarged and altered in later centuries. As timber-framed buildings tend to vary more by the area in which they were built than by date of building, I have combined discussion of them into a single section — see **The Timber-Framed Tradition**.

MEDIEVAL GREAT HOUSES

In the late Middle Ages, whilst the great landowners and other dignitaries of church and state continued to live in castles, the emphasis shifted from defensive measures to domestic comfort. Great improvements were made in existing castles — not least in the royal castles like those at Windsor and Winchester — and by the early 16th century, 'great houses', palaces rather than castles, began to appear. For some time they continued to retain the trappings of castles — battlements, etc to provide a spectacular background for tournaments and similar displays. The medieval 'great' house was, of course, not just the home of an individual and his family, anyone of authority in the land in the Middle Ages was supported by an army of retainers and dependants. As travel became easier, there was also much 'progressing' around the country by great nobles, accompanied, inevitably, by hosts of retainers. The great hall with its Saxon origins was still the most important domestic building in which even kings and princes led very public lives although this too began to change in the direction of greater privacy. Chapels too were important buildings even within castles and the same care and expenditure was lavished on them as upon parish churches in the later Middle Ages. Not all great houses were secular. Bishops and other high churchmen built themselves lavish palaces — the ultimate is probably Hampton Court which Cardinal Wolsey built at the very end of the period. Many of the bigger Oxford and Cambridge colleges were also built at this time and their plan and lay-out is typical of the great houses of the period.

By the late 15th century the need for greater comfort began to assert itself in Scotland as well and the Scottish castle began the slow transformation from fortress to tower house. Scottish lairds continued to maintain their defences until well into the 17th century and to continue to call their tower houses 'castles' until long after that. The late 16th century and early 17th century was the golden age of Scottish castles — a time when the prevailing influence was French rather than English — and some splendid tower houses were built in a distinctive Scottish style. They were tall — as many as six storeys — with thick walls, had battlements and small projecting corner turrets called bartizans, crow-stepped gables, decorated dormer windows, bases were plain without openings other than gun-slits. Craigievar near Aberdeen is an outstanding example. As in England, most of the grander castles were transformed in the late Middle Ages into palaces.

Plan: Rectangular with buildings arranged around a courtyard or quadrangle with the great hall flanked by its chapel, solar and parlour on one side of the hall, pantry and buttery on the other with the kitchens behind. The gatehouse, often quite elaborately 'castellated', was on the opposite side of the courtyard from the great hall. The remaining sides of the courtyard contained rooms for retainers and guests — and the retainers of guests.

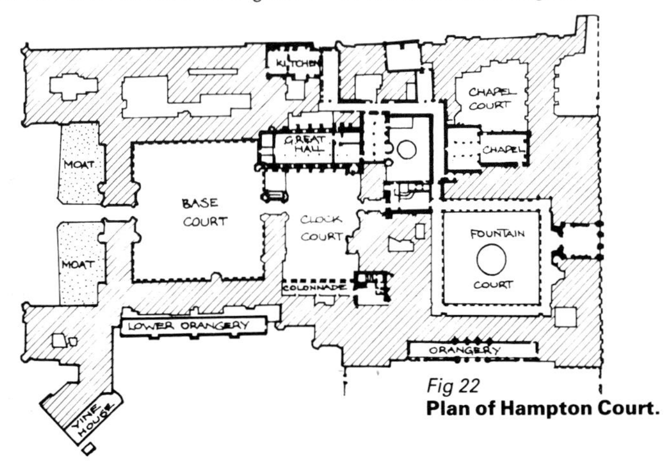

Fig 22
Plan of Hampton Court.

Above:
Herstmonceux Castle, East Sussex. The licence to crenellate was granted to the owner of Herstmonceux as late as 1440 and it is more of a mansion than a castle despite its apparent fortifications. It is, of course, built of brick, one of the first uses in Britain. It was partly dismantled in 1777 and faithfully restored in the 1930s. Note that the castle is symmetrical — a Renaissance feature.

Below:
Medieval mansions were built around courtyards entered through strong gatehouses. This is the courtyard at Herstmonceux. Originally there were four of them.

Below:
Leeds Castle, Kent. Once a royal castle, Leeds has been a mansion since the late Middle Ages but much of its medieval appearance dates from the 19th century. With removal of the curtain wall, the position of the central courtyard is clear.

Elevation and Walling: Walls were thick but not strong enough to withstand bombardment and there was an increasing use of brick in eastern England from the mid-14th century. Parapets were still battlemented, some walls had arrow slits to maintain the castle image. Many of the domestic buildings inside the stone or brick outer walls were timber framed. There was nearly always at least one tower — again in the castle tradition.

Roofing: There was an increasing use of baked tiles in the east and southeast, especially with brick walling, from the mid-14th century onwards. In the north and west, thatch, stone slates, lead, and oak shingles continued in use until the mid-16th century.

Windows and Doors: Openings are now much larger with flatter 'Tudor' or 4-centre arches. The large windows in the great hall and the chapel had tracery in the 'perpendicular' style and there were oriel windows on upper floor rooms. Some bay windows appear at the end of great halls late in the period.

Fireplaces and Chimneys: There was an open hearth fire in the centre of the great hall until the late 15th century when fireplaces and chimneys came into use first in solars and parlours.

Locations

Although they may have been altered subsequently, the following 'great' houses retain many medieval features of the date shown:

Scotland:

Castle Campbell, Central, 15th century, 17th century (SSS); **Aberdour Castle**, Fife, 14th century (SSS); **Stirling Castle**, Central, Great Hall, c1500 (SSS); **Cawdor Castle**, Highlands, 14th century-15th century, 17th century; **Dunvegan Castle**, Skye, 15th century-16th century, 19th century; **Urquhart**

Right:
In Scotland the transformation from fortress to mansion came later than in England. This is Crathes Castle, Grampian built 1553-96 — the large windows are later additions — it is typical of the French-inspired Scottish Baronial style, especially the bartizans.
John Mackay

Below:
Traquair House, Borders. Originally a royal hunting lodge and probably the oldest inhabited mansion in Scotland, Traquair was a tower house. It was enlarged in Baronial style during the reign of Charles 1 (1625-49). *John Mackay*

Castle, Loch Ness, c1509, ruined (SSS); **Dirleton Castle**, Lothian, 13th century, ruined (SSS); **Edinburgh Castle,** Great Hall, 15th century and 16th century; **Crathes Castle**, Grampian, 1553-96.

Wales:

Carew Castle, Dyfed, c1500; **Raglan Castle**, Gwent, 1445-68 (Cadw); **Beaumaris Castle**, Gwynnedd, c1400 (Cadw); **Tretower Court and Castle**, Powys, 15th century (Cadw); **Lamphey Palace**, Dyfed, 14th century (Cadw).

England:

Naworth Castle, Cumbria, c1350; **Skipton Castle**, North Yorkshire, c1535.

Midlands — **Stokesay Castle**, Salop, 14th century and 16th century (NT);

Kirby Muxloe Castle, Leicestershire, 1480-84 (EH); **Ashby de la Zouch Castle**, Leicestershire, 1464; **Haddon Hall**, Derbyshire, 16th century; **Tattershall Castle**, Lincolnshire, c1455 (NT); **Compton Wynyates**, Warwickshire, c1480-1528; **Broughton Castle**, Oxon, 14th century; Many **Oxford** colleges have medieval features, notably **New College**, 1380-87.

East Anglia — Many **Cambridge** colleges, notably **Queen's College**, c1465; **Oxburgh Hall**, Norfolk, c1485 (NT).

Southeast — **Penshurst Place**, Kent, 14th century; **Knole**, Kent, c1470 (NT); **Hampton Court**, London, c1514-36 (EH); **Eton College**, Berkshire, c1440; **Hever Castle**, Kent, 15th century; **Herstmonceux Castle**, East Sussex, c1441; **Windsor Castle**, Berkshire, gatehouse 1509.

Southwest — **Bishop's Palace**, Wells, Somerset, 13th century; **Winchester Castle**, Hants, Great Hall, 1235; **Winchester College**, 1382, 1481.

MEDIEVAL MANOR HOUSES

The line between the 'great' house and the manor house cannot be too finely drawn any more than can that between the landowner and the courtier. In general, however, we are looking at smaller houses built to house the lord of the manor and his family and servants, to serve as the administrative centre of an area and also as a court of justice — hence we often find the names 'hall', 'manor', and 'court' attached to them. Generally such houses were built with only the minimum of defences although moats and the licence to crenellate remained powerful status symbols for generations to come. Late in the period — by the early 16th century — quite often the military appurtenances were confined to an imposing gatehouse or to the frontage of the wings. Domestically, the manor house followed the open 'great' hall tradition of the larger houses. Most of the houses surviving from the early Middle Ages — there are said to be about 20 as early as the late 12th century are of stone, many with an undercroft on the ground floor and the open-hearthed hall on the first floor. By the mid-15th century, however, manor houses whether of stone, brick or timber-framed began to become standardised in plan — a single storey hall open to the roof with two-storeyed cross wings at either end forming the shape of the letter 'H'.

Plan: H-shaped, an open great hall with a raised dais at one 'upper' end, sometimes with a canopy. Behind the dais, doors or doorways go through to the lord's family's parlours and stairs to their solars or chambers. At the 'lower' end, a passage between front and back doors screened by a partition — the screens passage. Doors from the screens passage led into the buttery, the pantry and out to the kitchens which were usually external, stairs led to upper floor chambers separated from the lord's by the upper half of the great hall.

Elevation and Walling: Local materials were used for manor houses, stone in upland Britain and along the limestone belt, timber-framing in lowland areas, with an increasing use of brick in eastern counties in the 15th century when bricks became cheaper. Some castellated towers are found.

Above:
Ightham Mote, Kent. A perfect example of a moated medieval manor house, Ightham Mote was first built between 1340-74 and added to in subsequent centuries notably c1478, c1520, c1630 and in the 19th century. This view is from the southwest and shows the moat that surrounds the house, the 15th century west front with its three-storey entrance tower complete with oubliette; the south side with its timber-framed upper storey, with 15th century windows in the stone below, and above, multiple stacks of chimneys.

Below:
The Courtyard, Ightham Mote. From the gateway there is on the extreme right the great hall with its five-light 'perp' window; to its left is the solar with its oriel window and decorated barge boards, round the corner is the Tudor chapel built 1521-29. (There is another, older, 14th century chapel behind the solar.) In the far left corner is a staircase. The dog kennel is 19th century.

Roofing: Some variety but generally thatch with timber-framing, tiles and brick, flags or stone tiles with stone.

Windows and Doors: In door openings the Gothic two-centred arch of the 14th century and early 15th century gives way to the 'shouldered' (c1500) and 'four-centred' arch of late 15th century and 16th century. In windows, mullioned and shuttered windows (15th century) give way to multiple-light mullioned windows glazed with leaded lights under a squared bracket mould. Large windows in the great hall, small windows in ground floor of wings, bigger ones upstairs.

Fireplaces and Chimneys: A central hearth in the middle of the hall until the early 15th century, smoke louvres above. Fireplaces were introduced in the late 15th century, spreading rapidly in the 16th century with the introduction of brick. Fireplaces were built on the rear wall of the great hall at the beginning, later fireplaces were built into private rooms as well. Many late medieval brick chimneys were very ornate.

Locations

As with all survivals, the pure medieval manor house is extremely rare and almost all have been rebuilt in later periods.

Scotland:

In Scotland the tower house with slowly improving domestic facilities remained the typical residence of all ranks of land-owner from the king to the humblest Border laird until well into the 17th century when newer styles, usually influenced by the Renaissance, began to emerge (see **Tudor and Jacobean Houses**). The examples which follow are those of the smaller tower house of the medieval period which again have been enlarged and altered in later periods. **Arbruthnott House**, Grampian, c1522. **Craig Castle**, Tayside, a courtyard house early 16th century. **Claypotts Castle**, Tayside, late 16th century.

Wales:

Aberconwy House, Gwynedd, c1450 (NT); **Cochwillan Old Hall**, Gwynedd, c1400; **Ty Mawr**, Gwynedd, c1500 (NT); **Weobley Castle**, West Glamorgan, c1400 (Cadw).

England:

North — **Rufford Old Hall**, Lancashire, late 15th century (NT); **Markenfield Hall**, Ripon, North Yorkshire, 14th century; **Shibden Hall**, Halifax, 15th and 16th centuries; **Shandy Hall**, North Yorkshire, 15th century.

Midlands — **Southwick Hall**, Northamptonshire, 14th century; **Baddesley Clinton**, Solihull, Warwickshire, dates back to 1300 (NT); **Coughton Court**, Warwickshire, dates from 1409 (NT); **Billingborough Hall**, Lincolnshire, c1520; **Boothby Pagnell Manor House**, Lincolnshire, c1200.

East Anglia — **Baldwin Manor**, Swaffam Prior, Cambridgeshire, early 16th century; **Giffords Hall**, Suffolk, 15th and 16th centuries; **Fleming's Hall**, Bedingfield, Suffolk, c1550; **Lovell's Hall**, Terrington St Clement, Norfolk, 1543; **Elsing Hall**, Norfolk, c1460-70, restored 19th century.

West — **Lower Brockhampton**, Bringsty, H&W, 14th century (NT); **The Greyfriars**, Worcester, late 15th century (NT).

Southwest — **Bradley Manor**, Newton Abbot, Devon, 15th century (NT); **Cadhay**, Ottery St Mary, Devon, c1540; **Holcombe Court**, Holcombe Rogus, Devon, c1520-30; **Shute Barton**, Axminster, Devon, late 16th century (NT); **Athelhampton Hall**, Dorset, c1500; **Great Chalfield Manor**, Wiltshire, late 15th century (NT).

Southeast — **Beddington Place**, Surrey, c1530-40 rebuilt 1740; **Cowdray Park Gatehouse**, West Sussex, 1530-40; **Temple Manor**, Strood, Kent, 13th century; **Old Soar Manor**, Plaxtol, c1290 (NT and HBMC); **Ightham Mote**, Sevenoaks, Kent, 13th-17th centuries (NT); **Battel Hall**, Leeds, Kent, 14th century; **Wickham Court**, West Wickham, Kent, c1469; **Dorney Court**, Bucks, 15th century; **Hendred House**, East Hendred, Berkshire, c14th century.

Above:
Gainsborough Old Hall, Lincolnshire. This medieval hall was rebuilt 1470-84 after it had been burnt by the Lancastrian army and was enlarged in 1597-1600. This is the north side — notice the northeast tower and stair turret, the hall front with a chimney breast and stone-built bay window — 'perp' tracery.

Right:
Grevel's House, Chipping Campden, Gloucestershire. This is a medieval village house built c1390 by William Grevel, an ancestor of the Warwick family. Note the two-storey bay window with its 'perp' tracery.

The Timber-Framed Tradition

For centuries the main material for building the bulk of ordinary peoples' houses — which is what we mean by 'vernacular' — was timber. What we see today are the survivors of a style of building that has its origins in deepest antiquity, was used before the Romans and by them and evolved throughout the Dark and Middle Ages to reach its near perfection in the 15th and 16th centuries and then, inevitably to decline. Its history parallels exactly that of the steady reduction in the natural woodlands of these islands and in particular the availability of mature oak trees. When oak was cheap and plentiful many houses were built of it. As oak became scarcer in the mid-16th century and afterwards because of clearances, its use for charcoal-based iron smelting, in shipbuilding and in the demand for houses by a growing and increasingly prosperous population, it was steadily replaced by brick. Thus, the timber-framed houses we see today — apart from the modern 'brewer's' or 'stockbroker's' Tudor — date from a period rarely earlier than the 15th century or later than the 17th century, the bulk being 16th century — the century of the Tudors. Among the more humble dwellings, cottages and very small houses, few have survived earlier than the 18th century. There are, however, fewer historical variations of the style than there are regional variations and for this reason, it seems appropriate to deal with the entire tradition at this point in the book. It is also essentially an English tradition. In Scotland and Wales there are few survivals earlier than the late 18th century.

The type of house — or farm building — we are dealing with here is known as 'timber-framed' or 'half-timbered', the latter title deriving not from the fact that half the walls are wood and the other half brick or plaster but that the timbers used are halved, ie cleft. There are three main types of timber-framed buildings, each determined by the nature of the framing:

The 'Cruck' House: In this, grown, shaped or jointed timbers run up from the ground to the ridge to form a pointed arch like that found in early Gothic architecture. As in Gothic, cruck buildings carry the weight of the roof on pairs of such crucks set at bay intervals apart; the walls between the crucks carry very little load. Cruck houses are found mostly in the north, Midlands and west of England and in Wales, with the largest number in Hereford. A few are found in the southwest and virtually none east of a line from Chichester to Hull.

Post and Truss Construction: Akin to cruck in that the weight of the roof is taken by regularly spaced frames comprising strong vertical posts supporting stout roof trusses either triangular with a tie beam or set above framed arches which sometimes are mistaken for crucks. The weight of the roof is carried to the trusses by long horizontal timbers known as purlins and by the wall-plates running under the eaves and joining the tops of the posts. This form of construction can usually be recognised by the division of the longer walls into bays, the use of curved wind braces under the rafters and the projection of the end of the purlins at the gable ends. Often these purlins are linked with heavy collar beams and where there are two purlins, by two collar beams. These are not found in the south and east. There is sometimes a vertical post rising from the collar beam and running to the ridge known as a 'king' post; where there are two vertical posts supporting the purlins, they are known as 'queen' posts. Post and truss construction is more generally found in the midlands and north; rarely in the south and east.

Box-Framing: Here the thrust of the roof is taken by the walls, which are not divided into bays but have regular and substantial vertical timbering. The roof itself has simple rafters joined by collars near the apex. Often there is a collar-purlin — a single long timber joining all the collars together. This purlin may in turn be supported at intervals from transverse tie beams by what are known as 'crown' posts. Box-framing of this type is confined to the south and east as far north as York.

Above:
High Street, Weobley, H&W. Weobley boasts a remarkable variety of timber-framed houses — a cruck is visible in a house in front of the church, the inn on the left is box-framed, jettied and has a cranked tie beam and curved braces. The small square panelling is typical of the west and north.

Left:
Cruck-framed cottage at Weobley. Crucks are confined to the northeastern half of England and their history is a matter of continuing academic debate.

As always in this subject, generalisations have to be qualified — there are many variations of style and they overlap in individual buildings and in areas. In recent times, there have been many erudite and detailed studies of the carpentry of timber-framed buildings and the study of vernacular architecture is now a separate discipline which can only be touched on in a book of this type. It is not however short of literature — see **Bibliography**.

Plans: There are three main varieties of the open hall type:
Aisled: The roof span is extended by additional rows of wall posts and plates (known as arcade plates) within the building. Many aisled halls were built up to about 1400 in the southeast, later elsewhere; aisled barns were built as late as the early 19th century.

Above:
No 9 Castle Hill, Lincoln. Three gables, two jetties and another pattern of framing but still in the tall, close studded eastern style.

Left:
A half-timbered wing and the rest stone-built or stone-faced as befits a house on the very edge of the stone belt, the Broadway Hotel, Broadway, Worcestershire was originally a hall house — the hall in the middle — probably late 15th century and the stone dating from c1585.

Single-ended: A hall with a two-storey wing attached as a 'T' or 'L' shape, the projection is often just the jettying. There is a cross passage between the hall and the wing with doors leading to the pantry and buttery on the ground floor, the solar above. The fireplace is usually on the longer wall or at the open end of the hall. Stairs are in the wing. Kitchen is outside.

Double-ended: A hall flanked by two multi-storeyed wings, projecting on one or both sides or by jettying. The cross passage is at one end (the lower end) of the hall, leading to service rooms with chambers above. The other wing has parlours on the ground floor, and chambers above. The fireplace is on a side wall or an end wall. Stairs in both wings. Kitchens are outside.

Elevation and Walling: *Framing:* Regional variations: square panels with short straight braces between posts and wall plates with decorative timbers (stars, trefoils, cusping, etc) are found mostly in the midlands, the north and the west in 17th century; in the east and south, tall narrow 'perp' panels with curved braces rising from the sills; there is a tendency in the north to set posts directly on to the ground. The fashion for close 'studding' (ie timber uprights) and for the carved decoration of timbering came in the 16th century in the south and southeast. Later in the 17th century, the high cost of oak led to a return to large square panels without decoration. Timbers were left bare or lime-washed. (The blacking of timbers in timber-framed houses is largely a Victorian affectation.)

Infilling: Plastered wattle and daub dates from the 14th century onwards, it was replaced by brick nogging in the south and east in the 17th century but much is 19th century. Lath and plaster is also found and also dates from the 19th century. Local variations of infilling also include clay lump, chalk, cobbles, flint and stone. Houses were given white or colour wash using ochres, oxblood, etc. Whole houses were plaster covered in the 18th century in the southeast to hide unfashionable timber-framing. Houses were also refaced in brick or weather-boarded in the 18th and 19th centuries.

Mixed Walling: In areas of good building stone (eg Cotswolds) timber-framed houses in the towns and bigger villages had stone dividing walls, and rear walls, because of the fire risk. Sometimes only the front shows the timbering.

Jettying: The projecting upper storey known as the 'jetty' came in first in urban houses in the early Middle Ages to increase floor space, or strengthen the building or to protect the lower storey from rain, or to enable shorter timbers to be used — or all four, nobody really knows. The fashion quickly spread to the country and 'jetties all round' became fashionable in the late 15th century but went out of fashion during the 16th century. Regional variations include curved supports in the east and south, coving in the north west and tiled weatherings in the Midlands.

Roofing: From the early Middle Ages to the late 15th century, the majority of smaller houses were roofed with thatch, or oak shingles, but many have been subsequently re-roofed. Evidence of a former thatch can often be seen by weatherings — projecting ledges — on the walls and chimney stacks. Stone tiles were used from the Middle Ages in stone areas like the Cotswolds. Brick tiles were in use in bigger houses in the southeast from about 1500; smaller houses in the north and west were not tiled until the late 17th century. Pantiles were used in East Anglia from the 17th century and spread over eastern England by the 18th century. They were not used in the west except for barns. Slate tiles are usually a 19th century introduction. The line of the roofs of the centre and the wings is a clue to dating — higher eaves on the wings usually indicates additions and often a date earlier than c1400.

Windows: The earliest windows were in the casement style with wood mullions, unglazed but with shutters. Glass became cheaper in the late 16th century and larger windows, mullioned with leaded lights made their appearance. In the mid-16th century the introduction of chimneys allowed a

Left:
Great Dixter, Northiam. The hall and porch are very close-studded and built at a time when oak was abundant, c1475. (The bay windows to the great hall on the right were added in a restoration in 1910 by Lutyens.)

Left:
Weatherboarding or clapboarding is a form of timber cladding introduced in the late 18th century. It is largely confined to the southern and eastern counties where its use not infrequently hides a timber-framed house. These houses are in Tenterden, Kent.

floor to be inserted in the great hall and the tall hall windows were removed and replaced by smaller ones on each storey.

Doors: From the 14th to early 15th century, doorways had pointed arches in Early English Gothic style. The shouldered arch came in about 1500 and some examples of a depressed ogee or keel arch are also of this time. The Tudor arch dates from the late 15th century to the early 17th century.

Chimneys: Stone or brick chimneys were introduced in the mid-16th century usually as projections from one of the outer walls or at the cross passage end of hall. Early stacks were plain, later, in the 16th and 17th centuries, stacks were decorated by the use of moulded and carved bricks. Chimney pots were not used on smaller houses until the 19th century.

Stairs: In the Middle Ages access to upper storey was usually by a simple wooden ladder in smaller houses and these remained in use in some cottages until the 18th century. In larger houses, a spiral staircase was built into the side of the fireplace and chimney breast from about the mid-16th century. Framed newel staircases of the dogleg or well type came in from the late 17th century.

Timber-framed houses range from large mansions like Little Moreton Hall in Cheshire to tiny two-roomed cottages and all have their charm and interest. In a book of this sort it is possible only to look in detail at one specific type of timber-framed house that displays the main characteristics of the tradition, the Wealden House. Its design was widely adopted and variations of it, despite its name, are to be found all over the country (see **Wealden House**).

Locations

England:
North — MEDIEVAL: **Samlesbury Hall**, Lancs, 1350; **Wythenshawe Hall**, GM, 1475.
TUDOR & JACOBEAN: **Little Moreton Hall**, Cheshire, 1500 (NT); **Handforth Hall**, Cheshire, 1550; **Bramhall Hall**, Cheshire, 1575; **Adlington Hall**, Cheshire, 1581; **Gawsworth Hall**, Cheshire, 1600; **Treasurer's House**, York, 1650 (NT).

Midlands — MEDIEVAL: **Lord Leycester Hospital**, Warwick, 1383; **Stratford Grammar School**, Warwickshire, 1417. **Shakespeare's Birthplace**, Stratford, Warwickshire, 1450; **The Old Hall**, Gainsborough, Lincolnshire, 1450.
TUDOR & JACOBEAN: **Anne Hathaway's Cottege**, Warwickshire, 1500; **Hall's Croft**, Stratford, Warwickshire, 1525; **Mary Arden's House**, Warwickshire, 1525; **Cwmmau Farmhouse**, Brilley, H&W, 1625 (NT); **Upton Cresset Hall**, Salop, 1575; **Boscobel House**, Salop, 1625 (EH); **Blakesley Hall**, West Midlands, 1575.

East Anglia — MEDIEVAL: **The Priory**, Lavenham, Suffolk, 1450; **Little Hall**, Lavenham, 1450.
TUDOR & JACOBEAN: **Paycocke's**, Essex, 1500; **The Guildhall**, Lavenham, Suffolk, 1525 (NT); **Christchurch Mansion**, Suffolk, 1575.

London — TUDOR: **Whitehall**, Cheam, 1500.

South — MEDIEVAL: **Eyhorne Manor**, Kent, 1425; **Great Dixter**, East Sussex, 1450; **Pattydene Manor**, Kent, 1470; **Stoneacre**, Kent.
TUDOR & JACOBEAN: **Smallhythe Place**, Kent, 1550 (NT).

THE WEALDEN HOUSE

In the more prosperous areas of Sussex and Kent where the influence of London was strong, the architectural status symbol of the late 14th century and 15th century was a house with jettied upper floors and this is exemplified in a specific 'design' found most commonly in the Weald and hence known as the 'Wealden House'. It is however also to be found throughout the southeast and East Anglia and it was a style indicative of the prosperity of the yeoman farmer in the late Middle Ages. The style later found its way into other areas as a symbol of quality.

Plan: Rectangular with a central 'great' hall open to the roof flanked by two storied wings with jettied upper storeys all under a single hipped roof. At one end of the hall is the service wing and at the other, the solar wing, both with chambers above. The screens passage runs between the service wing and the hall in the usual manner.

Elevation and Walling: Because the hall is not jettied, it is recessed behind the jetties and the roof runs in an unbroken line from one end of the building to the other, the wall plate of the jetties also runs across the recess and is usually supported by arch braces from the jetties on both sides. Walling is usually timber-framed, with brick infill. Older houses may have some wattle and daub especially internally.

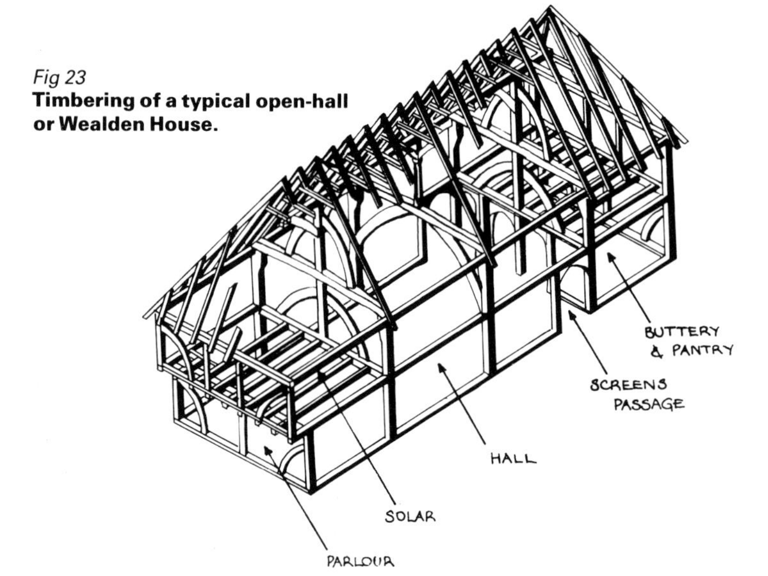

Fig 23
Timbering of a typical open-hall or Wealden House.

Above:
The Bell Inn, Waltham St Lawrence, Berkshire is a 'Wealden' house dating from the 14th century. 1 Great hall open to the roof recessed behind; 2 Two-storied, jettied wings with solar and parlour at one end, services — buttery, pantry at the other where 3 the screens passage runs across the house; 4 A hipped roof running in an unbroken line from one end to the other; 5 Fireplace and chimney put in in the 16th century on one wall of the great hall. This chimney has a small weathering at its base which suggests that at one time the house was thatched. It has, of course, also been rendered.

Roofing: A hipped roof sometimes with gablets and in thatch, tile or stone slab depending upon the location and date.

Chimneys: The central hall originally had an open hearth in the middle of the floor with smoke vents in the roof above. In the 16th and 17th centuries upper floors were usually inserted in the hall and a brick chimney was built against one of the walls.

Doors and Windows: Arched doorways, the shape of the arch is a clue to the date, two-centred (Gothic) and ogee arches are early, three and four centred, later. Doors which have survived are massive with heavy planks, studs and powerful hinges, some have iron grilles. Early windows are wooden with a single diamond shaped mullion without glass but with shutters running in grooves inside. Later ones have multiple mullions with casements of diamond shaped leaded lights.

Interiors: Some internal partitions were of wood panelling, occasionally with a built-in settle; there were also built-in cupboards often near the fireplace where things could be kept dry. Ceilings — especially after the insertion of floors into the 'great' hall, were heavily beamed and the beams were often moulded. The shape of the moulding and its stops are also a clue to date. Numerous small holes in ceiling beams indicate that a false flat ceiling had been fitted at one time — usually in the 19th century. Stairs in a house of this quality are usually in the form of a straight companion way in each wing but some spiral staircases alongside the chimney breast were put in when the fireplace was installed and the hall was floored in the 16th century.

Above:
The Crown Inn, Chiddingfold, Surrey was tile hung until the 1940s and is also a 'Wealden House', probably 15th century but could date back to 1383.

Below:
A fascinating variant on the 'Wealden' theme is this house in Weobley — was it one house or two? It is the Unicorn Hotel.

The Tudor and Jacobean Period, c1530-1640

This period begins when most of the major building was ecclesiastical and the dominating style we now call 'Gothic' had reached its peak with the evolution of the distinctive and uniquely English combination of vaulting, tracery and glass known as Perpendicular. The last and perhaps the supreme example of that style is to be found in the abbey church at Bath, begun in 1499 and not completed until 1616. The end of the Gothic era began during this period with the completion of Inigo Jones's Queen's House at Greenwich c1637, a superb first example of the Palladan style of Renaissance architecture in Britain (see **The Classical Era**). The century is thus one that marks the transition from a style that emphasised the vertical, the asymmetric and the rambling to one that stressed the horizontal, the balanced and the compact, and from one rooted in religion and shrouded in mystery to one founded on human values and the application of mathematics and science. It was also one of the most eventful and turbulent periods of our history. It began with a land divided into three separate and warring kingdoms wedded to the international church of Rome, largely dominated by powerful prelates like Cardinal Wolsey at Court and by influential monastic land-owners in the country at large. By the end of the period, the land was united under a single monarch, albeit uneasily, who was also head of the national Protestant church, again uneasily, and who was disputing power not with high priests but with a new class of secular magnates who had at least more claim than any of their predecessors to represent the bulk of the people. The monasteries had been dissolved, their lands dispersed and their buildings demolished or given over to other uses, many being rebuilt as country mansions by their fortunate recipients. After Henry VIII, however, there was little royal building. Queen Elizabeth built nothing except improvements to existing palaces like Windsor, preferring to progress from one courtier's house to another with her vast retinue — and the courtiers responded by building bigger and more elaborate houses. The country prospered and there had been an unprecedented boom in building in England and Wales — of houses, colleges and other public buildings but not of churches of which, following the Dissolution, there was a surfeit and many became derelict. It was a period too of intense and adventurous nationalism — the colonisation of the New World and the establishment of maritime power coupled with near isolation from Catholic Europe and the wave of new ideas from the south, notably from Italy where the so-called 'Renaissance' had begun in the 14th century.

The term 'Renaissance' means, literally, 'rebirth' or more aptly in modern terms 'born-again' and to thinkers and writers of the Victorian era who reintroduced the term, it was seen grandiosely as a new upsurge of the human spirit leading to the 'discovery of the world and of man' — a concept almost without bounds in time and influence. Latterday thinkers tend to limit the term to its artistic manifestations as a deliberate, even joyful, imitation of the classicial patterns of ancient Greece and Rome and conscious adoption of the values and standards of that era. All art was affected but the greatest impact was upon architecture and building styles. Here there was an abandonment of the Gothic style and a reversion to that of ancient Rome based upon a study of the ruins of that city and also upon the writings of a Roman architect and theorist, Pollio Vitruvius (c40BC). The dissemination of these Renaissance ideas and motifs in the late Middle Ages occurred largely through the work of itinerant Italian craftsmen and to a lesser extent from returning noblemen and others who had spent time in Italy and came back with pattern books. Such craftsmen were working in England as early as 1511 but their work was confined to adding Renaissance motifs in the decoration of essentially Gothic structures like Henry VII's tomb in Westminster Abbey, to Henry VIII's grotesque Nonsuch Palace (demolished in the 17th century)

Above:
Base Court, Hampton Court. The most complete example of a Tudor palace, Hampton Court was built by Cardinal Wolsey in 1514-26. In 1529 he gave it to Henry VIII (1509-47) who added to it. His Great Hall with its 'perp' window is on the left. With its proliferation of towers and turrets, battlements and pinnacles and total lack of symmetry, it is still a Gothic building.

Right:
In Scotland, James V (1513-42) rebuilt Stirling Castle with the help of French master-masons. This is the Great Hall — rather more symmetrical and with sculpted balusters based on German examples. *John Mackay*

and to Hampton Court. With the break from Rome, Italian craftsmen were discouraged and visits to Italy became politically hazardous. Links with the Continent were mainly through Flemish, French or German artists and craftsmen, many of them refugees fleeing Catholic persecution. Thus for most of the 16th century and early 17th century, the ideas of the Renaissance came to Britain tinged with French, German or Flemish overtones. But again, such influence was mainly decorative. The Elizabethan and early Jacobean period was one of spectacular high fashion and often extravagant and ostentatious individualism. Renaissance motifs and Flemish decoration were adopted as fashionable conceits — 'curious devices' copied from foreign books that were fun to incorporate into a house to make it 'busie and fantasticall'. Classical columns, medallions, and rounded arches were employed to embellish buildings that with their tall small-paned windows were still essentially 'perpendicular' in style. Indeed, following the widespread toying with classical motifs early in Elizabeth's reign, there was a marked reversion to the 'perpendicular' inspiration of Gothic in the design of houses built in the late 16th and early 17th centuries. Towers and turrets, high gables and tall windows came back into fashion as a last fling of the style that had held sway in these islands for 300 years.

The late 16th century also saw the arrival of the professional building designer who called himself 'architect' — a word and a concept unknown until that time. (The first use of the word 'architect' in English came in 1563.) Unlike the craftsmen builders — practical master masons and 'surveyors' — they were artists and draughtsmen from the outset and mathematicians and students of classical theory by training rather than masons or carpenters. Of the older school, the outstanding example is Robert Smythson (1536-1614) who helped to build Longleat, Woolaton, Hardwick Hall, and Burton Agnes and many more. Of the new school were John Shute (d1563) who wrote the first English architectural book and the greatest of them all, Inigo Jones (1573-1652) who brought the first true Renaissance classical architecture to England and whose work was to continue to have influence for the next 250 years.

During the Tudor and Jacobean period there was little variation in the architectural developments in Wales or Scotland although the Scots were more open to French Renaissance influence than the English in the rebuilding of their tower houses and castles.

From the foregoing, it is clear that most of the building during the Elizabethan and Jacobean period was domestic, either houses or public buildings. Some churches were built but the main influence of the period was upon the design of church interiors especially upon woodwork and highly decorated tombs, many of which survive to this day. At the very end of the period came Inigo Jones's seminal St Paul's in Covent Garden — completed in 1638, a revolution in church architecture on the very eve of the Civil War. There was also some military building. After his break with Catholic Europe, Henry VIII, fearing invasion, built a string of fortresses along the south coast from Gravesend to St Mawes and Pendennis, most of which still stand. Their main interest lies in the advance in their design over medieval castles in face of the steady improvement in artillery (see **Medieval Castles**).

Elizabethan and Jacobean Houses

As we have seen, the late 16th century and early 17th century was a period of great house building. Courtiers built vast mansions to proclaim their wealth, their prominence or their taste. Their 'great' houses are often known nowadays as 'prodigy houses' — Audley End, Longleat, Hatfield, Woolaton, Burghley, Falkland Palace, among them. As in every age, lesser mortals aped their betters and 'gentry' houses, in country or town, even some smaller farm and urban houses, adopted the style of the period. (And, of course, most vernacular building continued to be in the timber-framed tradition.)

Plan: The sun and the south wind were considered harmful until well into the 17th century and most houses of this period face north. One aspect of the design of Elizabethan houses which may or may not have Renaissance origins was the pronounced tendency towards a new symmetry in planning — very much a classical concept, unknown to the Gothic. As a result, designs began to move away from the traditional medieval 'H-plan' in favour of the 'E-plan' not because as was once believed the initial letter of the Queen's name was 'E' but to achieve symmetry. The older 'H-plan' house had the main entrance offset to the through passage at the screens end of the hall and the wings were often of different sizes as they had different functions. In the E-plan, the main entrance came in the centre of the hall and often had a porch to match the identical wings. At the same time, the enclosed courtyard with its protective gatehouse and surroundings wall attached to the end of the wings gave way to the detached gatehouse or to the 'frontispiece' or porch. In 'great' houses and some lesser, the long gallery became a feature, a combination of living room, art gallery, nursery and recreation room where families took refuge thoughout the winter.

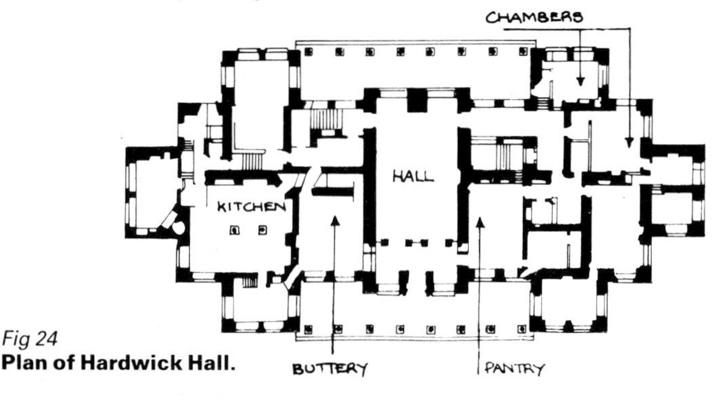

Fig 24
Plan of Hardwick Hall.

Elevation and Walling: Away from the stone producing areas, houses were increasingly built of brick — and the techniques and skills to produce highly ornamental brickwork have their origins in the Tudor period. Walling tended to be flat without the buttresses and deep window recesses of the 'Gothic'

Above:
Sutton Place, Surrey, an early Tudor mansion built c1520. It faces north and was originally a courtyard house but the north wall was removed in 1786. It has 'perp' windows but it is symmetrical — the doorway is in the middle of the hall. Like Hampton Court it has Renaissance ornaments in terracotta.

Below:
Woolaton Hall, Nottingham, the epitome of the 'busie and fantasticall' Elizabethan great house, Woolaton is symmetrical, rectangular in plan with four corner towers. 1 In the middle is the Great Hall, rising through three storeys and lit by clerestory windows; 2 Above it is the turretted 'prospect room' with traceried windows; 3 The upper storey of this south front is the customary long gallery running right across the house; 4 The windows are large and square, mullioned and transomed; 5 The chimneys are grouped and pinnacled. The storeys are of equal height and ornamented by classical pilasters divided by niches — the orders are, incidentally, used correctly.

Below:
Hardwick Hall, Derbyshire. That great Elizabethan, Bess of Hardwick, built her new Hall, 'more glass than wall' in 1590-97 when she was already 70. The master-builder was probably Robert Smythson. It is H-shaped in plan with stepped extensions. The main part of the house is two-storeyed, the wings and extensions are three-storeyed. The grid of mullions and transoms are a novel feature in the windows which by their size show a basement, a first storey and a deeper second. The drawing and dining rooms on the first floor with the state rooms including the High Great Chamber are on the second. Note the colonnade between the towers and the balustrading along the parapet.

Left:
In Scotland most building in this period tended to be either traditional or subject to French influence. This is the gateway to Falkland Palace, Fife, built in 1541, 'Scottish Baronial' in keeping with the castles of the time.
John Mackay

which with the great expanses of glass gives an almost 'cardboard' effect to some late Elizabethan houses. Other distinctive features are listed below.

Porch or Frontispiece: Many otherwise Gothic style houses have raised porches featuring the classical orders as decoration — often incorrectly. One also finds open loggias or colonnades upon the front and connecting the wings to the main part of the house.

Great Hall: Except in palaces and colleges with many occupants, the tendency by the end of the Elizabethan era was for the traditional open hall to be reduced to single storey height by the insertion of a ceiling/floor and for separate family dining rooms and parlours to make their appearance.

Shafts and Corner Turrets: Early houses often have octagonal shafts — similar to 'perpendicular' pinnacles and similarly decorated with carving. These were gradually replaced by octagonal corner stair turrets which at the end of the period gave way to larger square towers as the newel stair was replaced by the well staircase.

Gables and Finials: A pronounced skyline feature is the gable — crow-stepped, Flemish, scrolled and convoluted, squared or steeply pointed. In timber houses, there was the intricately carved or pierced bargeboard. Parapets, gable points and kneelers were crowned with vases, balls, circles, obelisks and a wealth of heraldic beasts.

Bay Windows: The late medieval oriel window gave way to the bay, semi-circular, square, angular, even pointed — and one above another.

Roofing: Steeply pitched roofs with parapets were the norm on stone and brick houses with the increasing use on the latter of baked tiles but stone slates, shingles and lead continued to be used. Thatch was almost universal for vernacular housing in the countryside but was strictly controlled in many towns.

Chimneys: One of the great delights of the Tudor era is its variety of tall chimney stacks in stone or brick — early ones twisted, diapered, fluted and embattled, later ones simpler but in clusters of an octagonal, square or diamond plan. In Jacobean times, arcaded rows made their appearance sometimes united by entablatures.

Windows and Doors: The area of windows gradually increased throughout the period but retained the narrow pointed 'perpendicular' style until late in the 16th century when the squared mullion and transom form of window was generally adopted. Thereafter came the vast areas of 'more glass than wall' that is a characteristic of the late Elizabethan era. Door and window heads were at first Tudor-arched but were gradually replaced by rounded heads and squared ones.

Other notable features:

External: Deliberately constructed gardens and ornamental parks were first introduced in the 16th century. Quite often, seemingly as part of that ornamentation, decorated and detached gatehouses within view of the main house became fashionable, the decoration, like that of the porch being in the classic style.

Internal: Richly carved and decorated fireplaces and chimney pieces are a feature, their design often based on classical motifs gleaned from imported pattern books. Wooden wainscotting or panelling was used to line the walls, parchemin or linenfold in the early 16th century gave way to simple rectangular panelling with raised mouldings. Moulded ceiling timbers with plaster infilling, sometimes heavily ornamented, gradually gave way to elaborate plaster ceilings and friezes covered with host of 'Emblemes'.

Locations

Scotland:

Linlithgow Palace, Central, 1534-41, 1618-20 (SSS); **Stirling Castle**, Central, 1540-2, 1594 (SSS); **Falkland Palace**, Fife, 1537-41; **Culross Palace**, Fife, 1597-1611 (SSS); **Kellie Castle**, Fife, 17th century and 18th century (NTS); **Castle Fraser**, Grampian, 1575-1636 (NTS); **Drum Castle**, Grampian, addition 1619 (NTS); **Graigievar Castle**, Grampian, 1610-26 (NTS); **Crathes Castle**, Grampian, c1553-95 (NTS); **Hamilton House**, Lothian, c1628 (NTS); **The House of the Binns**, Lothian, 1621-30 (NTS).

Wales:

St Fagan's Castle, South Glamorgan, c1580-86; **Raglan Castle**, Gwent, medieval, remodelled c1550-70 and 17th century (Cadw); **Llanfihangel Court**, Abergavenny, Gwent, late 16th century altered 1627. **Plas Mawr**, Conwy, Gwynedd, 1576-80.

England:

North — **Levens Hall**, Cumbria, tower houses remodelled as an Elizabethan mansion c1578; **Sizergh Castle**, Cumbria, medieval, additions mid-16th century (NT); **Chillingham Castle**, Northumberland, frontispiece, c1625; **Slingsby Castle** (ruined), North Yorkshire, c1620 by John Smythson; **East Riddlesden Hall**, West Yorkshire, 17th century (NT); **Oakwell Hall**, West Yorkshire, c1583; **Temple Newsham**, West Yorkshire, c1628; **Speke Hall**, Liverpool, 1490-1612 (NT); **Lyme Park**, Cheshire, c1570 (NT); **Burton Agnes Hall**, Humberside, 1601-10; **Burton Constable**, Humberside, c1600, 1760.

Midlands — **Benthall Hall**, Salop, 16th century (NT); **Wilderthorpe Manor**, Salop, late 16th century (NT); **Bolsover Castle**, Derbyshire, Jacobean fantasy castle, 1612-21, 1629-34, John Smythson (EH); **Haddon Hall**, Derbyshire, medieval house altered 16th century and c1600; **Hardwick Hall**, Derbyshire, 1591-97, Robert Smythson (NT); **Woolaton Hall**, Nottingham, 1580-88, Robert Smythson; **Thrumpton Hall**, Nottinghamshire, c1608; **Doddington Hall**, Lincolnshire, 1593-1600; **Marston Hall**, Lincolnshire, 16th century; **Gainsborough Old Hall**, Lincolnshire, late 15th century, 1500-36; **Charlecote Park**, Warwickshire, c1558, altered (NT); **Harvard House**, Stratford, Warwickshire, 1596; **Boughton House**, Northamptonshire, c1550, late 17th century; **Burghley House**, Northamptonshire, c1550-87; **Canons Ashby**, Northamptonshire, c1580 (NT); **Lyveden New Build**, Northamptonshire, c1600 (NT); **Chastleton House**, Oxfordshire, c1603. **Chavenage**, Gloucestershire, c1576. **Owlpen Manor**, Gloucestershire, c1540, 1616; **Snowshill Manor**, Gloucestershire,

Above:
St Fagan's Castle, South Glamorgan. An austere gabled E-plan house symmetrical on either side of the porch. It was built c1580 and was widely copied in South Wales over the next hundred years.

Below:
Chastleton House, Oxfordshire. A symmetrical, five-gabled house with flanking stair turrets with an emphasis on the vertical, similar in style but on a smaller scale to Smythson's Hardwick and Woolaton. It was built c1603.

Above:
Wilton House, Wiltshire. The original courtyard house built here c1560 was burned down and the south front was rebuilt in 1648 probably by John Webb with advice from the aged Inigo Jones. Horizontal rather than vertical it has all the attributes of the type of Palladian house that was to dominate the first part of the Classical Era.

early 16th century, later (NT). **Sudely Castle**, Gloucestershire, medieval castle extended c1572. **Grey's Court**, Oxfordshire, c1600, 18th century (NT); **Stonor Park**, Oxfordshire, c1600, late 18th century; **Hatfield House**, Hertfordshire, 1607-12, Robert Lyminge.

East Anglia — **Felbrigg Hall**, Norfolk, 1615-24 (NT); **Blickling Hall**, Norfolk, 1619-27 (NT); **Christchurch Mansion**, Ipswich, Suffolk, 1548-50, 1674; **Kentwell Hall**, Suffolk, c1560; **Melford Hall**, Suffolk, 1554, 1578 (NT); **Audley End**, Essex, begun 1603 (EH); **Layer Marney Tower**, Essex, c1520.

London — **Boston Manor**, Brentford, c1620; **Hall Place**, Bexley, 1538, 1556.

Southwest — **Cotehele**, Cornwall, late 15th century (NT); **Godolphin House**, Cornwall, early 16th century; **Lanhydrock**, Cornwall, c1620 with later additions (NT); **Trerice**, Cornwall, c1570 (NT); **Barrington Court**, Somerset, 1552-64 (NT); **Brympton d'Evercy**, Somerset, c1520, 17th century; **Montacute House**, 1590-1601 (NT); **Avebury Manor**, Wiltshire, c1557, 1600; **Corsham Court**, Wiltshire, 1582, 1760; **The King's House**, Salisbury, Wiltshire, medieval, 17th century: **Longleat House**; Wiltshire, 1567-80; **Westwood Manor**, Wiltshire, c1530, 1616 (NT).

Southeast — **Breamore House**, Hampshire, c1583 (restored); **The Vyne**, Hampshire, 1618-27, 1655 (NT); **Chenies Manor House**, Buckinghamshire, c1530; **Losely House**, Surrey, c1562; **Sutton Place**, Surrey, 1520-30; **Danny**, West Sussex, c1593; **Parham House**, West Sussex, c1577; **Glynde Place**, East Sussex, c1569; **Haremere Hall**, East Sussex, 17th century; **Michelham Priory**, East Sussex, medieval, 16th century; **Boughton Monchelsea Place**, Kent, 1567-75; **Cobham Hall**, Kent, c1580-1603, 18th century; **Godinton Park**, Kent, c1628, 19th century; **Knole**, Kent, medieval, 1603-08 (NT); **Sissinghurst Castle**, gatehouse, c1560 (NT).

THE CLASSICAL ERA, c1640-1840

The Classical style slowly replaced the Gothic throughout the Elizabethan and early Stuart periods and was to dominate the design of British buildings of all types for the next two centuries and continues to influence architectural thinking to the present day. Indeed, for most of the Western world and not a little of the Eastern, the Classical 'orders' *are* architecture. As the Greek philosopher Plutarch said of the buildings of the Acropolis in Athens: 'They were created in a short time for all time'. In other words, a style of temple building which evolved nearly 3,000 years ago in a small Mediterranean country has continued over the centuries to epitomise for most people all that is elegant and beautiful in what is man's most creative and useful art. (I have said 'most people' because throughout history there have been those who have preferred the Gothic, often on religious as much as aesthetic grounds, seeing that style as the Christian opposite of the pagan Classical. In fact, the two styles are, as we shall see, not entirely unrelated.)

So far in this book, we have examined two distinct architectural styles — the 'Romanesque' of the Anglo-Saxon and Anglo-Norman periods and the 'Gothic' of the Middle Ages. Both these styles were based on the use of arches, the one rounded, the other pointed. (The word used is 'arcuated'.) But it takes some skill and sophistication to throw arches, round or pointed. It is simpler to take four long stones or pieces of wood, stand two upright and make a pointed arch of the other two — or simpler still to take three and make a sort of table — two legs and a top — like the ancients did at Stonehenge. We would call that a 'post and lintel' structure — there are plenty around the house today — and the word used in this case, is 'trabeated'. Now the ancient Greeks were much more primitive than the Romans when it came to building technology — the basic principle of their structures was 'post and lintel', not arcuated. So the essence of the Classical style is that of posts holding up flat tops. But, as Churchill might have said, 'some posts, some flat tops'. For the Greeks were sublime artists with a sense of style, form, proportion, elegance and harmony that has yet to be equalled. Their posts became 'columns', their flat tops, 'entablature'. They made their columns in careful proportion of diameter to height, elegantly tapering them upwards, and usually mounting them on moulded plinths or pedestals, they put mouldings on the base and at the top — the 'capital' — of the shaft which they often fluted. Sometimes they added carving to the capital as well. Their flat tops or 'entablatures', they

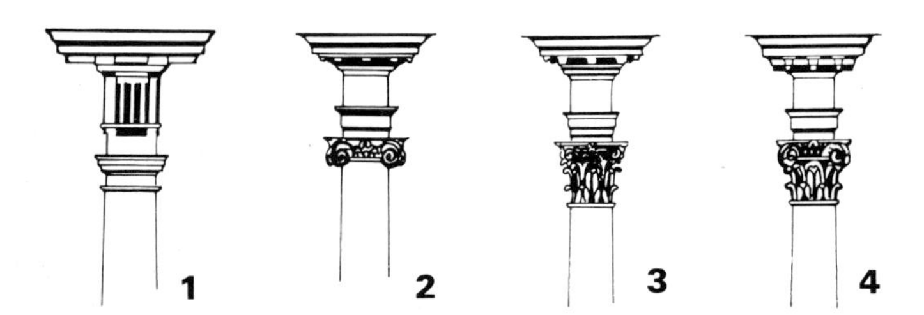

Fig 25
The Classical Orders: 1 Roman Doric; 2 Ionic; 3 Corinthian; 4 Composite.

also shaped, moulded and carved. And of course, being Greeks, they had words for all these things — words like 'astragal', 'torus' and 'scotia'. (If you are interested, you can find all these words in one of the reference works but you don't need to know them to appreciate classical architecture. And to my mind they tend to make what is an essentially straightforward subject unnecessarily complex.) Also being Greek and therefore logical, they matched the proportions and level of moulding, carving and decoration of the columns with those of the entablature and set out a series of such matched columns and entablatures ranging from the plain to the highly decorated. These groupings later became known as the 'orders' of Classical architecture and there were three of them to begin with — 'the strong, the elegant and the rich' or, as the Greeks may not have put it, the Doric, the Ionian and the Corinthian.

But these 'orders' were derived from archaeological sources by the Romans and later scholars and the classical orders are now reckoned to number five: the Tuscan, the shortest, plainest and the stubbiest (six diameters tall); the Doric, taller (eight diameters), fluted with decorated entablature; the Ionic, taller still (nine diameters), fluted with more moulding and a distinctive scroll (called a volute) carving at the capital and dentils (small square blocks) along the cornice; the Corinthian, slightly taller (ten diameters), fluted with acanthus leaf carving at the capital, slightly more elaborate entablature but still with dentils; finally, the Composite, a combination of the Ionic and the Corinthian with both scroll and leaf carving at the capital; the most elaborate and luxurious of all, it evolved after the

Above:
Not a Greek temple but, of course, the British Museum, built 1823-47 (Smirke). Fluted Ionic columns, dentiled cornice, sculpted pediment.

Right:
The Roman triumphal arch — or how the Romans built a rounded, barrel-vaulted arch into a simple Greek post and lintel: Corinthian pilasters on the outside, Tuscan pillars under the arch. This structure is repeated in many forms in Classical buildings of all types. The arch here is at Wilton House, Wiltshire and was built c1759 by Sir William Chambers.

Above:
Banqueting House, Whitehall, SW1. Part of James I's ambitious plan to rebuild Whitehall Palace in 1619, Inigo Jones' Banqueting House brought Palladian Classical architecture to the heart of London for the first time. It is built of Portland stone and has two floors and a basement, all are rusticated. The first floor has Ionic columns and pilasters, the second Corinthian. The first floor windows have pediments on consoles, alternately segmental and straight, those on the second carry a simple entablature on consoles. The building is also in Palladian proportions — in effect a double cube. (It was refaced in 1829 by Sir John Soane.)

Renaissance. There are also two versions of the Doric — the Roman which puts the column on a plinth and the Greek Doric which has no plinth. It is, however, the essence of classical architecture — the feeling, tone and tempo that a complete building conveys to the onlooker. The various orders are thus seen to have certain sensual characteristics — the Tuscan and the Doric, essentially masculine and for use in buildings like military academies, prisons and churches dedicated to the more rugged male saints. By this token, the Corinthian is feminine, the Ionic androgynous.

The Greeks used their 'posts and lintels' mainly to build temples and meeting places, mostly rectangular buildings with rows of columns holding up the eaves of a pitched roof. Thus at either end there would be a triangular gable which again could be moulded, carved and decorated in keeping with the order being employed. This triangular gable we know as a 'pediment' and it is often used decoratively.

These then are the basics of the classical style and its 'orders'. If you want to build something like a Greek Temple — say a church, a town hall, a bank or a major museum, then you can use them in much the same way that the Greeks did and there are many buildings of this type to be found in major cities, not only in this country but throughout the world. Most of them convey a sense of balanced proportion, dignity, elegance and ageless refinement that reflects not only upon those who created them but — as was intended — upon the institutions, authorities or individuals who had them built. But such temple-like buildings are applicable only to a few limited uses. So what if you want to use the 'orders' to convey the same feelings about a country house or palace, a cathedral, or an amphitheatre? You can of course, build your houses, palaces and public buildings in just the same way that you always have, given a few alterations for changes in local fashion and taste, and then stick on bits of column and entablature and pediment as a decoration. This, as we have seen, is what the Elizabethans and Jacobeans did, apart that is from Inigo Jones, but this is a long way short of 'classical' architecture. There you have to start with the basic proportions of the buildings themselves, their balance and their symmetry and ensure that all parts form a harmonious whole. Then you can apply the 'orders' as part of the structure to achieve the effects you want. And once again, there are some basic 'rules'.

These rules were not enunciated by the Ancient Greeks themselves but by the Romans who adopted and adapted the principles to create their own version of classical architecture. Its major contribution was that it achieved a harmonious marriage between the rounded Roman arch and vault and the column and entablature of the Greeks — ie between arcuated and trabeated structures. (The best example is the Roman triumphal arch, doggerel copies of which formed the basis of 'Romanesque'.) The Romans also did new things with the columns themselves whilst still retaining the basic 'orders'. They introduced the detached column with a wall behind and the entablature above; the three-quarter column, partly buried into the wall, and half columns similarly buried, and the built-in square flat column, still conforming to the proportions, mouldings and carving of the order, we call a pilaster. Another Roman innovation was in the spacing of columns where they established five standard spacings ranging from 1½ to 4 diameters, and in

Right:
St Paul, Covent Garden, WC2. Simple Tuscan columns without plinths, supporting a plain frieze and a pediment with projecting timber beams provide an imposing church porch. It is the prototype of Classical churches, chapels and meeting places all over the world and was built by Inigo Jones 1631-38.

Left:
Lindsey House, Lincoln's Inn Fields, WC2. Built in 1640, Lindsey House was one of the earliest town houses in London built with a rusticated base and giant order pilasters — note, too, the fenestration. Another prototype, its attribution to Inigo Jones is uncertain.

their grouping into pairs, trebles or quadruples. The Romans also used bricks and cement which meant that unlike the Greeks, they could build rounded structures like barrel vaults and domes.

We know all this because a Roman architect, Pollio Vitruvius (c40BC), set down what he saw as the basic principles of the style in the only major treatise on the architecture of the ancient world which survived until the end of the Dark Ages. His 10 books, translated into a variety of languages, exercised a great influence upon European builders and architects from the early 16th century onwards. Vitruvius' writings were, however, obscure and lent themselves to a variety of interpretations by architects of the time, including such notable figures as Michelangelo (1475-1564), Sebastiano Serlio (1475-1554) and above all of Andrea Palladio (1508-80). There thus emerged what were in effect, two schools of classical architecture — a pure and rather rigid classicism, and variations on the classical theme which grouped together are called 'Mannerism' — in the manner of classical building but not adhering to all its tenets. (We shall come across this word again when examining the various periods.)

Andrea Palladio was one of the greatest of Italian Renaissance architects. He made a deep study of the works of Vitruvius and of the ruins of ancient Rome. (Greece by this time was lost behind the minarets of the Ottoman Empire.) He interpreted the classical tenets in a uniquely elegant and artistic style which he applied to palaces, churches and especially to domestic buildings like his celebrated Villa Rotunda, Vicenza (1550-51). He also published his own books on classical architecture and it was the influence of his ideas upon the English architect, Inigo Jones, that brought the Classical style to these islands in the shape of Jones' Queen's House, Greenwich, (1629-35) and his Banqueting Hall, Whitehall (1619-22). The Palladian style of classicism thus established was to maintain its hold on British architecture until the 1820s but as we shall see, all manner of Mannerism was also to play its part.

When we come to look at classical buildings, there are several habitual usages that it is useful to know about besides the 'orders' I have outlined above. Here are some of them:

Pediments: Pediments can come in all shapes and sizes — small ones over doors and windows, large ones actually serving as eaves. They can be curved — ie segmental — or 'broken' where the sides end below the apex, they can be 'open' — spanning a break in the entablature, or they can be broken and 'scrolled'.

Consoles: Brackets in the shape of S-shaped scrolls deeper at one end than the other and used vertically as mounts for statues, etc or inverted as a sort of buttress.

The 'tempietto': Circular temple with columns supporting a circular entablature decorated to match the order but usually with balustrading above it. Used to support domes, for porticos, for mausoleums, and in miniature on steeples and towers.

The 'Giant Order': Also known as the 'Colossal' order, introduced by Michelangelo. It refers to columns — or pilasters — that extend through several storeys.

'Rustication': A method of giving the stones of a building a rugged, rough effect to convey solidity. Usually done by cutting deep grooves between the stones on the lower storey.

'Venetian Window': A triple opening with a wide arched centre flanked by two narrower openings with lintels. Sometimes all three are included within an outer arch.

Cubes and Double Cubes: Symmetry and proportion are intrinsic to classical architecture. Palladio laid down that to achieve harmony, the long and short sides of a room should bear a simple arithmetical relationship to each other and also to the height. Each room should also be in proportion to its neighbours. Thus we get, for example, a 'single cube' room, say 5m long, 5m wide and 5m high, next to a 'double cube' — 10m long, 5m wide and 5m high.

Aedicule: A niche in a wall intended to act as a shrine and containing a bust or statue, often adorned with a pediment, columns or pilasters.

The Stuart Period, c1642-1725

The convention of relating building styles to dynastic periods of history whilst useful, has to be interpreted rather freely when it comes to actual dates. We are dealing here with the period of the Civil War and the Commonwealth which followed it when there was little building of any sort, the Restoration of 1660 and the dazzling reign of Charles II, the brief episode of James II and the 'Glorious Revolution' of 1688, the arrival of Dutch William and Stuart Mary and on through William III's reign to that of Queen Anne who died in 1714 and, inevitably, a few years on into what is strictly the Georgian period.

There were three main architectural influences, all stemming to some extent from Inigo Jones' innovations in the early part of the 17th century:

(a) The development along Jonesian lines of the Elizabethan-Jacobean style with its Dutch and Flemish overtones by practical master-builders up and down the country who did not employ architects but took their patterns from illustrations of what was happening around the capital. This style, nowadays known as 'artisan mannerism', lasted from about 1630 until well into the 18th century.

(b) The continued 'naturalisation' of the Palladian classical style by Inigo Jones' successors, a variety of 'architects', amateur and professional. Notable among them — his assistant John Webb (1611-72), through Sir Roger Pratt (1620-84), Hugh May (1621-84), William Talman (1650-1719) and above all that great genius, Sir Christopher Wren (1632-1723). In Scotland, the classical style was introduced by Sir William Bruce (1630-1710) and a master mason, James Smith (c1645-1731).

(c) The use of the classical orders in a rather undisciplined and exuberant

manner by architects like Sir John Vanbrugh (1664-1726), Nicholas Hawksmoor (1661-1736) and Thomas Archer (1668-1743), often known as the English version of the much more voluptuous continental 'Baroque'. (Also copied by local craftsmen and known as 'Builders' Baroque'.)

That word 'Baroque' is one of those which means different things to different people. Its derivation comes from the Portuguese word *barocco*, meaning a pearl that is not perfectly round. Like the word 'Gothic' it also embraces a wide range of art forms from painting through architecture to interior decoration often uniting all three in a single design. The use of the word to describe a building style in the United Kingdom generally implies large scale, complex compositions, curved forms, exuberant decoration, and rich materials. Vanbrugh's Blenheim Palace and Castle Howard probably qualify; Wren's St Paul's, perhaps does not. On smaller buildings it implies a grandiloquent use of the classic orders. (Compared with the 'Baroque' of the Continent, however, British baroque is restrained and disciplined — just as in the Middle Ages, our Gothic never became 'flamboyant'.)

This was also an age of great artistry and craftsmanship in building and decoration — the exquisite wood-carving of Grinling Gibbons (1648-1721), the magnificent ironwork of Jean Tijou and the panel and ceiling paintings of

Left:

The English 'Baroque' style — large scale, complex, curvaceous, exuberant, rich. West Front, St Paul's Cathedral (1675-1711) — aedicules, rounded arches, tempiettos and a double portico of two temple fronts one above the other and both of the same (Corinthian) order. It has been said that Sir Christopher Wren intended to use the 'giant' order but stone large enough could not be produced.

Above:

South Front, Castle Howard, North Yorkshire (1700-30). Sir John Vanbrugh and Nicholas Hawksmoor were responsible for both Castle Howard and Blenheim Palace. This south front has giant order Corinthian pilasters, rustication, etc but the addition of the dome is the 'Baroque' feature.

Sir James Thornhill (1676-1734), Antonio Verrio (1639-1707) and Louis Laguerre (1663-1721) among others, add lustre to many of the great buildings of the period.

During the Stuart period, there was a good deal of building of country houses following the Restoration, of churches following the Great Fire of London in 1666, of public buildings and of urban houses and of 'villas' — small country houses without much land within easy reach of a town. We shall look at the main characteristics of each of these categories separately: country houses, churches and urban houses.

Above:
Northwest Front (Great Court), Blenheim Palace, Oxfordshire (1750-22). Here is the 'giant order' in the main portico supporting a huge pediment decorated with the Marlborough arms, a fantastic roof line and Doric colonnades everywhere.

Below:
State Apartments, Hampton Court Palace (1689-1702). Built in brick for William and Mary by Wren and Talman, this garden front displays all the essential characteristics of Wren's domestic style we shall see repeated in smaller settings although it was originally intended to have a dome. Compare it with Lindsey House (page 100).

Stuart Churches

With the enormous legacy of medieval churches — possibly as many as 9,000 to serve a population of under five million — there was comparatively little church building in most parts of Britain, with the exception of London, during the period between the Dissolution of the monasteries c1539 and the early 19th century. Until the Restoration in 1660, what churches were built were usually in a rather spare perpendicular Gothic style with only the occasional use of classical motifs as decoration. Once again, the change from Gothic and hybrid mixtures came with the designs of Inigo Jones. His simple church of St Paul's in Covent Garden (1631-33) with its temple proportions, Tuscan portico and pediment was to become the prototype for thousands of churches and chapels of all denominations throughout Britain and America in the centuries that followed. More immediately, in the Stuart period, its design was to be one of the influences on Sir Christopher Wren and his associates in the design of St Paul's Cathedral and of the 50 or so London churches which were rebuilt after the Great Fire of 1666 between 1670 and 1676. The Reformation of the Anglican church was also an influence against the older style of Gothic church with its often ill-lit nave, its aisles behind huge piers, its massive screens and its gloomy chancel. The Protestant liturgy of the Restoration period required churches where the congregation could both see and hear the service from the altar, the lectern and the pulpit

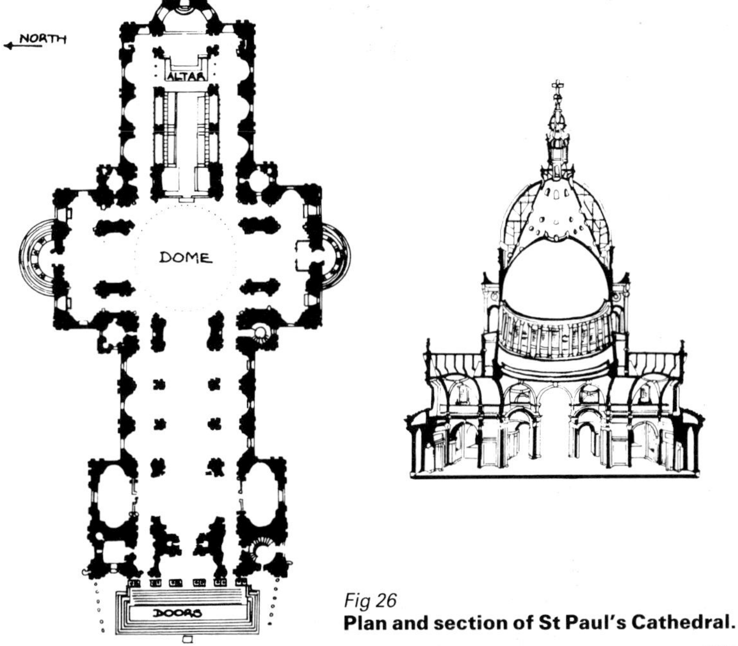

Fig 26
Plan and section of St Paul's Cathedral.

Above:
St Paul's Cathedral. Wren's masterpiece comprises four main parts, the choir seen here on the right, the dome and the crossing in the centre, the nave with its complicated twin towers on the left, and the west front. It is of two storeys but the upper storey is blind, the windows being replaced by aedicules. The walls are rusticated and pilastered. The crowning achievement is the great dome which in effect is a 'tempietto' on a grand scale. Note how every fourth column engages a supporting pier with a niche.

and Wren's task was to produce new churches that were, as he put it, 'convenient auditories'. And as the Nonconformists grew in strength from about 1730 onwards, they built their churches in a similar 'auditory' style.

Not all the 55 'Wren' churches were designed in detail by the master himself. They were largely the work of local craftsmen working to plans produced to suit the site concerned by Wren in his office as Surveyor General. Some years later Wren was also to produce the design of the spires. These 'Wren' churches were then themselves to become models for further church building during the Stuart period, notably the 'Commission' churches built between 1710 and 1730. Here the leading architect was Nicholas

Hawksmoor, Wren's pupil, who developed the now fashionable 'Wren' classical style in his own distinctive manner as did his contemporaries like Thomas Archer (1668-1743) and James Gibbs (1682-1754) who spread the style to America. As always, there were a host of other provincial architects and craftsmen who built 'Wren' style churches throughout England and Wales. In Scotland, the onset of classical church architecture was slower than in England and Wales and did not gather full pace until the late 1750s.

The main characteristics of Stuart or 'Wren' style churches are as outlined below.

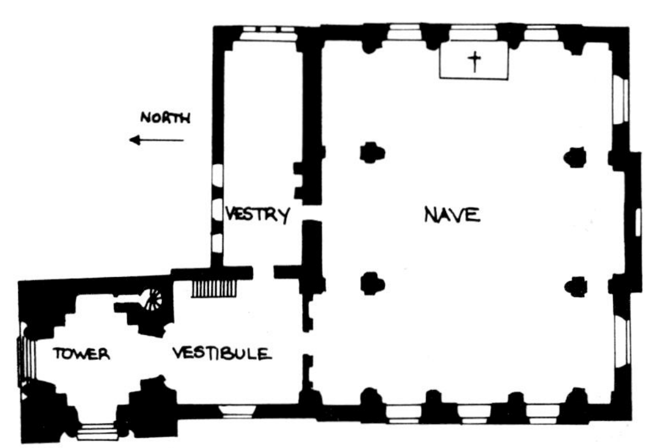

Fig 27
Plan of a typical Wren 'convenient auditory' (St Mary-le-Bow).

Plan: Basically rectangular but often adapted to fit the site available. Not all have choirs or transepts, the altar at the east end is often contained in a salient rather than a chancel. The nave is basically a hall with or without aisles sometimes with galleries above for extra seating but with a full view of altar, lectern and pulpit. Variations include cruciform churches within a basic rectangle or square, and some octagonal churches. There was great emphasis on the entrance tower and steeple, sometimes at the west end of the nave, sometimes to one side, sometimes two towers with steeples.

Elevation and Walling: Two-storied walling in the classical mode — two rows of windows of different sizes behind 'giant order' pilasters or columns. There is classical decoration of the frieze and cornice. Porticos with a pediment or in the rounded 'tempietto' style with balustrading are frequent. Towers are usually squared with the use of orders to various stages, usually ending in balustraded parapets, sometimes with pinnacles, and a steeple above.

Roofing: Usually a simple pitched roof behind a parapet with balustrading. Limited use of domes over crossing in cruciform churches — notably St Paul's Cathedral and St Stephen Walbrook.

Doors and Windows: Doorways are large and impressive; windows are often on two levels — small, sometimes of the bulls-eye type, along the lower level, larger at the second level, usually under rounded arches. Some use is

Left:
St Clement Dane's, Strand. A Wren church built 1680-82, the steeple was by James Gibbs in 1719-20.

Right:
St Mary le Strand, Strand. One of Gibbs' own churches, built 1714-17.

made of dormer and bulls-eye windows at the third, clerestory stage. Windows were of rectangular panes of clear glass with very fine leaded glazing bars — stained glass is largely a Victorian intrusion.

Spires: Of immense variety — ascending in a succession of diminishing stages and employing all the devices of both classical and gothic decoration. Wren and his successors gave London a skyline of unique beauty at that time.

Material: One unifying factor was the use of Portland limestone for all the churches, introduced for the first time by Wren.

Interiors: Generally plain in structure but with elaborate plaster work on the ceilings, capitals and covings. Woodwork was also good — box pews, elaborate pulpits under impressive testers. (Unfortunately, most classical churches were raped by the Victorians in an excess of zeal for the Gothic — see **Victorian Churches**.)

Locations

The vast majority of the Wren style churches are to be found in London and the most obvious example is that unique expression of Wren's genius, St Paul's Cathedral, which has, of course, all the characteristics I have outlined above. (That I have not dealt with it individually is not to diminish its importance but merely to emphasise that this book is less about specific buildings, more about styles.)

Scotland:

Tulliallan, Fife, 1675; **Hamilton**, Strathclyde, 1730, William Adam; **Lauder**, Borders, 1673, Sir William Bruce.

Wales:

Dolgellau, Gwynedd, 1716.

England:

North — **Holy Trinity**, Sunderland, T&W, 1719; **St Mary**, Stockton, Cleveland, 1712.

Midlands — **St Modwen**, Burton on Trent, Staffordshire, 1726, Francis and William Smith; **St Alkmund**, Whitchurch, Salop, 1712; **Holy Trinity**, Minsterley, Salop, 1689; **St Mary's**, Ingestre, Staffordshire, 1676, Sir Christopher Wren; **St Philip**, Birmingham, WM, 1715, Thomas Archer; **All Saints**, Gainsborough, Lincolnshire, 1744, Francis Smith.

East Anglia — **All Saints**, North Runcton, Norfolk, 1713, Henry Bell; **Old Meeting House**, Norwich, Norfolk, 1693.

London — Among churches designed by Sir Christopher Wren, the following are important examples although many of them had to be restored after being bombed in WW2: **St Paul's Cathedral**; **St Stephen**, Walbrook — the domed precursor of St Paul's 1672-87, steeple 1717; **St Peter's**, Cornhill, galleried, 1675-81; **St Clement Dane's**, Strand, 1680-82; **St James's**, Piccadilly, 1676-84; **St Vedast**, Foster Lane, baroque, 1695; **St Bride**, Fleet

Street, 1670-84, spire 1701-03; **St Dunstan in the East**, Eastcheap, only the Gothic spire survives.

Churches by Nicholas Hawksmoor: western towers, **Westminster Abbey**, 1734; **St George**, Bloomsbury, 1716-31; **St Mary Woolnoth**, Lombard Street, 1716-27; **Christchurch**, Spitalfields, 1716-31.

Churches by Thomas Archer: **St Paul**, Deptford, 1713-30; **St John**, Smith Square, 1714-28.

Churches by James Gibbs: **St Martins-in-the-Fields**, 1722-26; **St Mary le Strand**, 1714-17.

Southwest — **St Charles the Martyr**, Falmouth, Cornwall, 1662-64; **St George**, Tiverton, Devon, 1714-33, John James (1672-1746); **Congregational Church**, Frome, Somerset, 1707.

Southeast — **St Catherine**, Wolverton, Hampshire, 1717; **St Mary Magdalene**, Willen, Buckinghamshire, 1680, Robert Hooke; **All Saints**, Oxford, Oxfordshire, 1720, Henry Aldrich.

Below:
All Saints, Gainsborough, Lincolnshire. The 'Wren' style reached the provinces by the mid-18th century but this church built 1736-44 by Francis Smith of Warwick owes more to Gibbs. All the windows, for example, have the distinctive 'Gibbs surround'. In this case the medieval 'perp' spire was left standing.

Stuart Country Houses

As we have seen in earlier chapters, in medieval times, major country houses were built around courtyards. During the Tudor period, these courtyards began to be reduced to wings — the 'E-plan' house. In Jacobean times, these wings began to become shorter and in the Stuart period we see the emergence of the country house without wings at all. Not, of course, that this happened suddenly, at once or everywhere but it does give us a way of classifying country houses of the period as well as the others of size and derived architectural style. At one end of the scale we have the massive Vanbrugh palaces like Blenheim, Castle Howard and Seaton Delaval with their huge wings and courtyards and their baroque style. At the other we have the small square, rather plain 'Queen Anne' or 'Wren' house without any wings at all. Like the 'Wren' church, the 'Wren' house was to be adopted as a design throughout the English-speaking world — a truly livable house in towns as well as in the country. In between these extremes are numerous houses displaying a variety of plans and characteristics depending as much upon the whims of the owners and the wiles of the craftsmen who built them as upon any clear-cut architectural style. One of the attractions of Stuart country houses lies in detecting the various influences that have contributed to their design — a Dutch gable here, an Ionic portico there, and pillars and pilasters everywhere. Most of them, however, are likely to have these following features in common.

Plan: A rectangular central block with or without integral wings. The 'double-pile' plan where two rows of rooms are separated by a central corridor running the length of the house was also introduced. The traditional 'great hall' becomes the staircase hall with a vestibule and the servants' hall is moved to the basement. Principal rooms are now on the first floor.

Elevation and Walling: Two main storeys set above semi-basement, the latter rusticated, with pronounced string course between storeys. Bold eaves cornice, hipped roof above with attic dormer windows. Roof sometimes flat-topped with balustrading above the dormers and capped by a decorated cupola. Early houses have little decoration except stone quoins, and along the cornice and window and doorcases. Later houses, especially those tending towards 'baroque' have pilasters, often 'giant' order, supporting a bold cornice below the third (attic) storey with a parapet above to hide a hipped roof often with balustrading along the parapet. There is often a central pediment over the entrance front above a slight forward break in the wall often with supporting pilasters. The majority of houses were built of brick in a variety of colours. Bricks were also rubbed or carved to form pilasters, etc.

Windows: Until the end of the 17th century some houses still had lead-glazed transom and mullion casement windows. They were replaced — literally — by sliding sash windows, a Dutch invention, c1685. Sashes were at first held up by pegs, later by weights inside the 'boxing'. Stuart sash windows have heavy glazing bars and their boxing is sometimes visible from

Left:
In Scotland, the modernisation of old castles and tower houses continued throughout the period. This is Lennoxlove, Lothian at one time the home of Charles II's mistress, the Duchess of Lennox and Richmond. It was enlarged and remodelled by Sir William Bruce, between 1672-77.

Below:
South Front, Ham House, Richmond. Originally this was a Jacobean H-plan house built in 1610. It was altered in 1673-74 when the space between the south arms of the H was filled in and the facade was extended by the outer bays. The canted bay windows were formerly at the end of the wings. The windows would also have been mullioned and transomed but were replaced with sashes in the 18th century when the third storey Venetian windows were put in.

outside. (Window Tax was introduced in 1696 and not repealed until 1851 which explains some blank windows in Stuart and Georgian houses.) Window cases were sometimes moulded and pedimented with triangles or segments. Enlarged, artificial and decorated keystones are a feature of baroque houses.

Doors: Main doorways are approached by a flight or flights of steps, called perrons, often elaborate in baroque houses. Doorcases, pilastered and pedimented with a 'Gibbs' surround (alternating large blocks like quoins). Large wooden hoods, often shaped like shells, and supported by carved consoles or trusses are a feature of the period. Some porticos are found in baroque and Palladian houses. Glass was first used in doors during this period. Decorative ironwork for gates and railings is also a feature.

Interiors: Stairways, still with landings, have longer flights, moulded handrails, massive strings, Dutch-style turned balusters. Panelling — large rectangular panes with bolection (ie raised) moulding. Ceilings — simple geometric shapes formed by heavy enriched mouldings on plain ceilings. In the grander houses, elaborately painted ceilings and panels depicting scenes from classical mythology. Fireplaces — rather plain mouldings with panels above.

Gardens: The court garden walling is opened up by wrought iron railings and screens so that the house could see and be seen. This period saw the beginnings of 'landscape gardening' — putting a house in an impressive setting.

Locations

Scotland:

Brodie Castle, Grampian, c1660 (NTS); **Glamis Castle**, Tayside, c1675; **Drumlarig Castle**, D&G, c1691, J. Smith; **Dalkeith Palace**, Lothian, c1700, J. Smith; **Dumbarton Castle**, Strathclyde, c1700 (SSS); **Lennoxlove**, Lothian, c1675, Bruce; **Palace of Holyroodhouse**, 1671-79, Bruce.

Wales:

Erddig, Clwyd, c1675, T. Webb (NT); **Tredegar House**, Gwent, c1675; **Trewyn Court**, Gwent, c1692.

England:

North — **Nunnington Hall**, North Yorkshire, c1680 (NT); **Wallington House**, Northumberland, c1688 (NT); **Beninborough Hall**, North Yorkshire, 1716, Thornton? (NT); **Castle Howard**, North Yorkshire, 1726, Vanbrugh, Hawksmoor; **Capesthorne**, Cheshire, 1726, F. and W. Smith.

Midlands — **Woburn Abbey**, Bedfordshire, c1600, Flitcroft, Inigo Jones; **Sudbury Hall**, Derbyshire, c1670 (NT); **Ashdown House**, Oxfordshire, c1675, (NT); **Belton House**, Lincolnshire, c1688, W. Winde (NT); **Dudmaston**, Salop, c1675 (NT); **Upton House**, Warwickshire, 1695 (NT); **Calke Abbey**, Derbyshire, 1703 (NT); **Blenheim Palace**, Oxfordshire, 1716, Vanbrugh, Hawksmoor; **Chatsworth**, Derbyshire, 1707, Archer; **Hanbury Hall**, H&W, c1700 (NT).

East Anglia — **Wimpole Hall**, Cambridgeshire, c1730, Gibbs, Flitcroft (NT); **Peckover House**, Cambridgeshire (NT); **Kimbolton School**, Cambridgeshire, 1708, Vanbrugh.

London — **Ham House**, Richmond, 1674 (NT); **Fenton House**, Hampstead, 1675 (NT); **Kensington Palace**, 1690, Hawksmoor (DoE); **Hampton Court Palace**, 1702, Wren and Talman (DoE).

Southeast — **Uppark**, West Sussex, 1690, Talman (NT); **Squerryes Court**,

Kent, 1686; **Petworth**, West Sussex, 1696 (NT); **West Green House**, Hampshire, 1715 (NT); **Owletts**, Cobham, Kent, 1684 (NT); **Swallowfield Park**, Berkshire, 1678, Talman.

Southwest — **Kingston Lacey**, Dorset, 1663, Pratt (NT); **Dyrham Park**, Avon, c1700, Talman (NT); **Anthony House**, Cornwall, 1720, Gibbs? (NT); **Bowden House**, Devon, 1704.

Above:
A copybook Wren-style country house, Uppark, Sussex was built c1685-90 and the architect was William Talman. It is built of brick with stone dressings and apart from the pediment over the centre and the doorcase, is sparing in ornament. Note the dentiled cornice and pediment.

Left:
Winslow Hall, Winslow, Buckinghamshire. An urban house in a country town, probably the precursor of the 'villa', Winslow is almost certainly by Wren himself, c1699-1702. Built of locally baked bricks, it has a basement for kitchens and offices, two main storeys and a half storey; seven bays wide, the centre set forward and pedimented, open segmental pediment over the doorcase, hipped roof, four-panelled oblong chimney shafts.

Stuart Town Houses

Although mansions standing in their own grounds continued to be built in London similar in style to the winged 'great' houses built in the country — Kensington Palace and Ashburnham House (Westminster) are two of the few survivors — the Stuart period brought major changes to urban domestic architecture in both the 'large' and the 'small' categories of town house.

The compact, square, brick-built 'Queen Anne' or 'Wren' style house with its tall flat elevation and absence of wings made it highly suitable as a town house fronting a street, or a cathedral close or as a villa at the edge of a small town or village. There are many hundreds of them still to be found all over Britain (and the United States) with dates ranging from the mid-17th century to the early 19th century — and the style was revived vigorously by the Edwardians. This is one of the main domestic architectural legacies of the Stuart era but of equal importance is that of the terraced street and with it, the formal square.

Until the mid-17th century, most town houses outside the stone belts were built in the traditional timber-framed style, facing or side-on to the alley or street in unplanned warrens. Many, timber, stone or brick, had thatch roofs which is why fire was an ever-present threat. Building regulations to reduce that fire risk and to some extent the overcrowding around London were introduced by the early Stuart monarchs. But there was little in the way of town-planning until the Duke of Bedford's developments of the Covent Garden piazza — of which Inigo Jones' St Paul's church was a feature — with its terrace of brick-built houses came in 1630. After the Great Fire of 1666, although Christopher Wren's wonderful master plan was rejected, the Rebuilding Act of 1667 laid down standards for houses in London that were later adopted by municipal authorities throughout the United Kingdom. This Act was effective because not only did it spell out details of construction, it also appointed inspectors to see that its rules were carried out. The Act of 1667 was later modified by one of 1707 (which inter alia confirmed the Window Tax) and by a further Act in 1774 which we shall consider later (see **Georgian Town Houses**). Some knowledge of the first two acts is useful in dating terrace and detached houses in London and in detecting the styles in other places where they may have been introduced decades later than in the capital. In other words, our celebrated 'Georgian' terrace house, lived in and loved by perhaps as many as a million families even today, is really a Stuart innovation. These are the main stylistic implications of the 1667 Act:

(a) Houses would be built in terraces along both sides of a street.

(b) Four classes of house were envisaged: three classes and sizes of terrace house, the size being determined by the status of the street each faced; one class of houses standing in their own grounds.

(c) The smallest terrace type, facing narrow streets, had two storeys, a cellar and an attic as all had; the second sort fronting bigger streets or the Thames, had three storeys — the main living room on the first floor similarly, the third, facing wide major thoroughfares had four storeys — again with the main living room on the first floor, this time with a balcony. Detached houses were mostly two-storied.

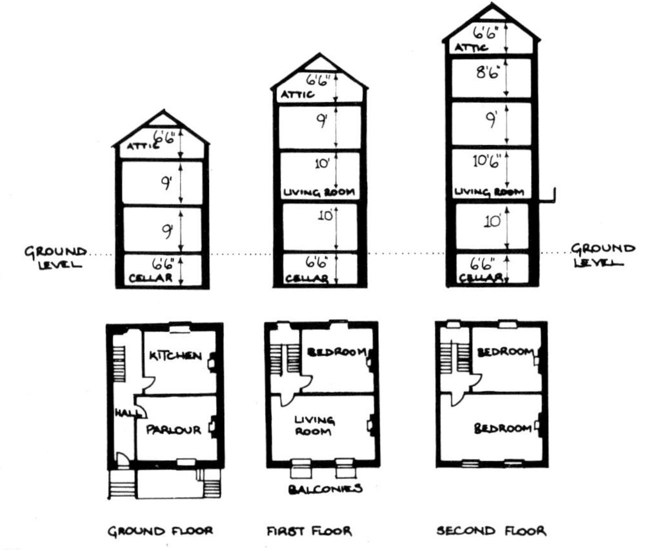

Fig 28
Standard types of houses as laid down in the London Building Act of 1667 and later copied throughout the country.

Below:
Moving down the scale, formerly Oxton Prebend 1, now Cranfield House, Southwell, Nottinghamshire, a splendid example of the smaller urban 'Queen Anne' or 'Wren' house and built c1709.

Above:
Pallant House, Chichester, West Sussex. Built c1712, probably craftsmen's 'Wren' — the main details are correct but it is not an organised design. The doorcase is oversized and the dodos on the gateposts are said to be bad shots at ostriches.

Below:
Queen Anne's Gate, SW1. London terraced houses built c1704 of brown brick with stone banding. One dentil cornice appears to have survived and notice the intricately carved door surrounds and canopies. These are four-storied houses fronting a broad street vide the Building Acts of 1667 and 1707.

Above:
And further still, this pretty pair of early 18th century houses, Nos 6-7 Castle Hill, Lincoln, brick with stone quoins and segmental pediments over the stone doorcases.

(d) The Act laid down the height of storeys — 9ft or 10ft (2.7-3m) and the size of the houses — 24ft (7.3m) square for the most part, some small ones had only 12ft (3.6m) frontage, the bigger types were often much deeper.
(e) As a fire precaution, the use of timber in building was strictly controlled but it was permitted for window frames, cornices and doorcases. Roofs were steeply pitched with clay tiles or slates. Detached houses often had attic dormers.

The Act of 1667 permitted window frames and doorcases to be fitted flush with the walls. That of 1707 did two things. First, it banned wooden eaves cornices so that roofs were ever after hidden behind parapet walls above brick or stone cornices, second it required that door cases and window frames be set back a minimum of 4in from the face of the wall. These two changes are usually seen as marking the transition from the 'Stuart' to the 'Georgian' town house. Again, although these changes were also adopted in the provinces, their significance for dating purposes outside London is unreliable.

The Georgian Period, c1725-1840

The early years of the 18th century were full of historic and dramatic change for these islands. Marlborough's victories at Blenheim and elsewhere culminated in the Peace of Amiens in 1713, Queen Anne's death in 1714 led to the establishment of the Hanoverian dynasty and in the process brought the Whigs to power until 1783. There was an upsurge in national self-esteem and, especially after the first Highland rising of 1715, a reaction against all things Stuart, Roman Catholic and foreign, particularly French. In architectural style there was a powerful movement away from the 'baroque' of Blenheim and St Paul's in favour of a return to the 'pure' style of Palladio as interpreted by the great — and British — architect, Inigo Jones. This new movement, led by Lord Burlington, was to dominate English architectural thinking until the 1750s with an almost religious fervour. It was sustained from several sources besides the national distaste for the 'affected and licentious' work of the French and Italian baroque. First, in the whole field of art, literature and philosophy, the ideas of a new rational enlightenment were beginning to hold sway — this was the age of John Locke and Alexander Pope — and with it a pronounced tendency towards moderation and harmony and away from ostentation and display. Second, the publication of successive volumes of Colen Campbell's *Vitruvius Britannicus* in 1715, 1717 and 1725 not only glorified Inigo Jones' Palladianism (and, not unsurprisingly, Campbell's as well) they also provided every fashion-conscious potential house builder throughout the land — client or contractor — with a singularly attractive pattern book. Architecture at the time was a subject of great popularity among the educated classes and a further boost to the passion for the Palladian style came from the first publication in English of Palladio's own *Four Books of Architecture* between 1715 and 1720 by the Italian architect Giacomo Leoni (1686-1746). The publication of these major works led in turn to the appearance of a spate of detailed instruction and pattern books that master masons, joiners and bricklayers could offer to clients up and down the social scale. Indeed, it has been said that the 18th century was the age of copybook architecture. Added to these influences was that of the aristocratic 'Grand Tour' which became fashionable again with the coming of peace in Europe. The 'Grand Tour' was an essential part of the education of rich young Englishmen and invariably took a year or more. It usually covered the major sites of classical antiquity in France and Italy and served to reinforce a young man's belief in the values of a Graeco-Roman golden age in whose languages, literature and philosophy he was already well versed by his exclusively classical education. When, after about 1750, it became possible to extend the 'Grand Tour' into Greece itself, it was a major influence in bringing in the movement for 'Greek Revival'.

The 18th century was a period of growing population and prosperity based on commerce and mercantile trade as Britain's maritime power expanded and trade followed the flag. In 1700 the population was around five million, total trade less then £10 million. By 1800, the population had reached 10 million and was to be 20 million by 1850. Trade in 1800 was over £40 million.

Left:
What is called 'Bristol Baroque' c1730 — the south side of Westbury House, Bradford on Avon, Wiltshire. Note the three orders of pilaster and the broken pediments of the centre bay. The 'Queen Anne' style continued to be popular in the provinces until well into the Georgian period.

Right:
In contrast, Gibbs' style Palladianism in Winson Manor, Gloucestershire c1740.

The main beneficiaries of this prosperity were the merchants and bankers who made up an educated middle class that was rich, fashion conscious, architecturally aware and 'upwardly mobile'. It was this class that in emulation of its social superiors created the heritage of superb smaller Georgian country and town houses and villas we still enjoy. Relatively few churches were built — mostly in the 'Wren' style but the pervasive good taste of the governing classes of the time is still apparent in many a bank, town hall, high school, hospital, prison — yes, prison, and theatres up and down the land. Town planning had begun at the end of the 17th century with the various London Building Acts. They were applied not only in the capital in developments like St James's and Bedford and other squares, their tenets were applied to places like Bath (from c1727), and Edinburgh (from c1766) as well as many smaller places like Inverary (c1743) and Blandford Forum (c1734) being rebuilt after major fires. Town planning continued on the grand scale late in the period in such developments as Nash's Regency London and fashionable 'spaws' like Buxton and Cheltenham.

The Palladian phase which covers the reigns of George I and George II is usually known as 'Early Georgian' — c1715 to 1740. Reaction to Palladian dominance then began to set in as various architectural savants began to take a renewed and experimental interest in styles of the past — the Gothic of the Middle Ages, with the opening up of Greece to travellers, the Grecian — and also of the orient, Chinese and Indian. There was no sudden and dramatic change but architects were in effect being gradually freed from what had been the Palladian strait-jacket and able once again to adopt and adapt freely the styles of the past and add to them a distinctive style of their own. Outstanding in this were the firm of Robert and James Adam and the 'Adam style' predominated from c1750-80. Its characteristics were the use of stucco and distinctive, colourful but delicate decoration internally — especially of ceilings — within rather severe but detailed exteriors. Again there followed a reaction — inevitably a reversion — to a Grecian form of Palladianism — by more traditional architects and building in this 'Late Georgian' style which in places continued until c1820. But stucco had come to stay as had cast iron and a new generation of genuinely professional architects began to employ them with a new freedom in individual styles based on the imaginative use of ideas from the past and from abroad — Gothic, Grecian, Chinese, Italian, Indian — in a supremely elegant and varied fashion we now call 'Regency' and which we shall examine separately (see **Regency Period**).

Below:
Based on Palladio's 16th century Villa Capra ('Rotunda') near Vicenza, and on other villas by Scamozzi, Chiswick House, Chiswick was designed and built by Lord Burlington between 1725-29 and ushered in the long reign of strict Palladianism. This is the southern entrance front with its elaborate stairways to the Corinthian portico. The ground floor is vermiculated — an elaborate form of rustication — and houses offices and a library, the first floor has the staterooms grouped around an octagonal saloon under the dome. They were decorated by William Kent to designs based on Inigo Jones.

Above:
Duff House, Banff, Grampian. Scottish Palladianism with a touch of the Baroque in motifs from Versailles, from Wren and Vanbrugh and built 1735-39. The architect was William Adam (1689-1748), father of the Adam brothers who themselves later broke the Palladian mould. Note the pedimented Corinthian centre-piece, the corner towers and the perron stairway. *John Mackay*

Below:
Blandford Forum in Dorset was rebuilt after a disastrous fire in 1734. One of its Georgian glories is the church of SS Peter & Paul built 1733-39 and designed by John and William Bastard.

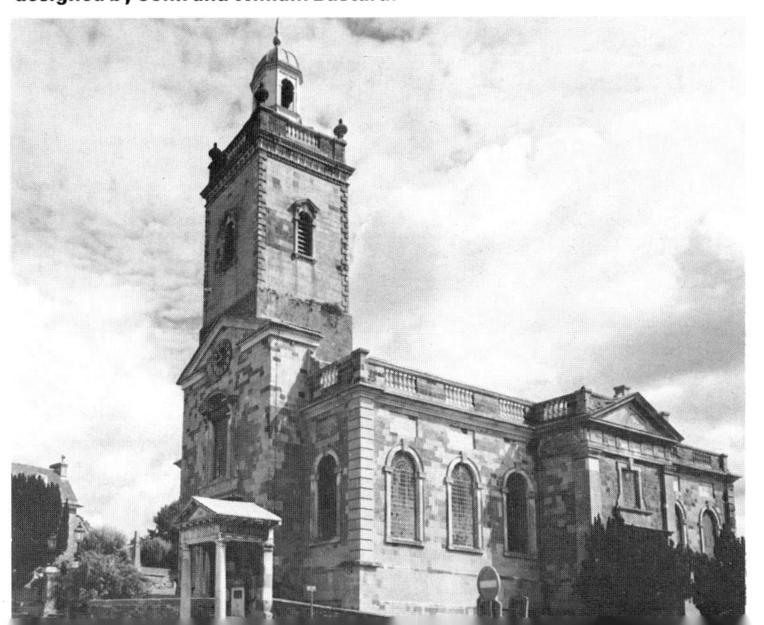

Georgian Country Houses

EARLY HOUSES AND VILLAS, c1720-60

The Palladian movement which dominated the early Georgian period was largely originated by Colen Campbell (1676-1729) who designed a number of Palladian-style houses, the most noteworthy, Wanstead House (1715, demolished 1824) and Stourhead, Wiltshire (1720). It was, however, the first volume of his book *Vitruvius Britannicus* which appeared in 1715 which attracted the attention of the Whig aristocrat, Lord Burlington (1694-1753) on his return from the Grand Tour. Burlington became Campbell's client and pupil and later returned to Italy and bought many of Palladio's drawings. He also brought back with him the painter William Kent (1685-1748) who later became both an architect and landscape gardener. These three men were the driving force behind the Palladian movement although Campbell quarrelled with Burlington before he died. Burlington himself designed and built his own archetypal Palladian villa at Chiswick (1723-29), Kent helped with the interior and laid out the garden. Also associated with Lord Burlington in the early days of the Palladian movement was James Gibbs (1682-1754) whose *Book of Architecture* (1728-39) was one of the most influential of a host of pattern books. Notable for its doorcase designs — including the famous 'Gibbs Surround' — it is believed to have inspired the design for the White House in Washington.

Palladian designs thereafter dominated architecture throughout the United Kingdom for country houses and villas of all sizes until the last quarter of the 18th century. In England and Wales, besides those named above, the main exponents of the style were: Henry Flitcroft (1697-1769); George Dance, the elder (1700-1768); Sir William Chambers (1723-96); Launcelot 'Capability' Brown (1716-83), the celebrated landscape gardener; Giacomo Leoni (1686-1746); Roger Morris (1695-1749); James Paine (1717-80) and John Carr (1723-1807), mainly in the north and the Midlands, Sir Robert Taylor (1714-88). In Scotland, the Palladian style (with baroque overtones) was first used extensively by William Adam (1689-1748), father of Robert, James and John and founder of the family firm. It was continued by James Clark and Sir William Chambers.

The main characteristics of a Palladian style country house are shown below.

Plan: Rectangular central block with central bays set forward on the main and rear faces, either standing alone or with quadrant walls running out to pavilions.

Elevation and Walling: Three main storeys, low basement, deep second, narrower third storey, central bays with pediments and supporting columns or pilasters from the basement. A hipped roof with dormers behind a parapet, sometimes balustraded. The ground floor rusticated and surmounted by a string course; a pronounced eaves cornice. Walls were usually brick built and stuccoed with the occasional use of stone for trimming.

Right:
North Front, Marble Hill, Twickenham (1723-28). Designed by Henry Herbert, the heir to Wilton House, and Roger Morris, Marble Hill is in the strict Palladian style of Chiswick — rusticated lower storey, deeper first floor, narrower second, Ionic pilasters and dentiled pediment.

Below:
Marchmont House, Borders. A highly individual Palladian house — notice the severe Venetian windows in the wings — built 1750-54. The architect was Thomas Gibson.

Roofing: Stone tiles were gradually being replaced by slate tiles from Cornwall and Leicestershire.

Chimneys: Unknown to Palladio — some architects created ingenious devices for smoke dispersal but the plain, slim tall stacks on either side of the hipped roof became the norm. Chimney pots were introduced at this time but some were sunk into the stack.

Windows and Doors: Sash type windows with mutiple panes, small and square in the basement and third storeys, larger and taller on second storey with some Venetian windows behind balconies. Windows were usually set in simple architraves with or without pediments or decorated keystones. The main entrance on the first floor is approached up a perron stairway in larger houses, or through a simple cased door in the basement in smaller houses.

Interiors: A columned entrance lobby and some family rooms — dining rooms, parlours, etc in the 'rustic' ie the lower storey; the main 'public' rooms including a two-storey cube or double-cube 'great room' (the medieval great hall in a later guise) and the major bedrooms on the second floor, other bedrooms and upper half of the 'great room' on the third. Sumptuous internal decoration using classical motifs — rooms divided by columns and entablature, pedimented door cases, elaborate and gilded plaster work on walls and ceilings and surrounded panels either painted themselves or framing paintings. Elaborately carved and columned marble chimneypieces with panels and paintings above. High relief classical ornament including sculpture.

Above:
Georgian villas also have Palladian pretensions — Old Bank House, Blandford Forum, c1731.

Left:
A house in Llansawel, Dyfed, probably not built until c1800.

Right:
Osterley Park, Isleworth. Originally an Elizabethan mansion built around a courtyard, Osterley was completely remodelled by Robert Adam between 1761 and 1780. Only the Tudor corner towers remain. The main rooms are on the first floor as is the entrance with its curved perron.

LATE GEORGIAN COUNTRY HOUSES (c1760-1800)

By the time Lord Burlington died in 1753, the Roman-based Palladian style he had fostered was also going out of fashion and the remainder of the 18th century was dominated by two architects — William Chambers (1723-96) and Robert Adam (1728-92) — both Scotsmen and bitter rivals. Chambers was the traditionalist, a founder member of the Royal Academy who was permitted by George III to use his Swedish knighthood. He is remembered only for two of his buildings — the Chinese Pagoda (1761) in Kew Gardens which reflected the current public interest in Chinoiserie, and his grand government office block, the enormous Somerset House (1776-86) in London. His style here was English Palladian with overtones of French neo-classicism, but very much in the traditional Roman mould. Robert Adam was an innovator of near genius and although he was also a self-publicist of 20th century capabilities, his elegant architecture, interior decoration and designs for furniture have gained him a reputation rivalling, if not eclipsing, that of Sir Christopher Wren. The 'Adam Revolution', as it was known, was really the introduction of a wider range of classical themes than those prescribed by Palladio, non-Roman as well as Roman — decorative motives from Pompei (then recently excavated), from discoveries in Greece and Asia Minor and especially what nowadays epitomises the 'Adam style' those called 'Etruscan'. These are flat decorations in strong colours, reddish-brown, black and yellow and based on ancient Greek vases. (Josiah Wedgwood copied them and called his factory Etruria after them.)

The latter half of the 18th century also saw the first beginnings of two great architectural revivals that were to flourish in the 19th century — the Gothic and the Greek. Horace Walpole (d1797) the novelist and letter-writer built his house at Strawberry Hill, Twickenham, in the 'Gothic Taste' and there were others like it but they were built mostly for fun and for 'follies', like Chambers'

Left:
Adams' greatest innovation is the Ionic portico spanning the courtyard entrance now raised to the level of the first floor. Notice the 'Adam-style' decoration of the pediment and the portico ceiling.

Below:
Hatchlands, Surrey. A very plain Palladian house of startling vermilion brick, Hatchlands was built 1756-57 and probably designed by the owner, Admiral Boscawen. Its internal decoration was Robert Adams' first commission after his return from Italy.

Pagoda. The Greek style was brought to Britain by two architects who visited ancient sites in Greece and brought back drawings which they published as *The Antiquities of Athens* in 1726 — James 'Athenian' Stuart (1713-88) and Nicholas Revett (1720-1804). Their actual building work was, however, very small. More prolific in a neo-Classical but highly individualistic style was Sir John Soane (1753-1837).

This period too was the time of the 'Picturesque' fancy — the idea that formal gardens were to be replaced by an ordered wildness that might have come out of a landscape painting — more specifically out of a landscape painting by the 17th century painters Claude and Poussin. So dead trees were planted, sham ruins — Greek, Gothic or Chinese were built where they could be viewed from the house — all to make Nature imitate Art.

Above:
Further Gothic — and here with a touch of Tudor — the refronting of the Sacrista Prebend, Southwell, Nottinghamshire, c1775 with windows to match the 'perp' in the minster.

Above:
The Georgian style in its purest form, The Old Manor House, Chiddingfold, Surrey, c1762.

Right:
This was also the age of the folly. Here is one of them — Leith Hill Tower, Surrey built in 1766 to raise Leith Hill to 1,000ft and make it the only 'mountain' in southeast England.

Although Robert Adam himself sought to give his buildings 'movement' by producing 'an agreeable and diversified contour' through the addition of curved quadrant colonnades, impressive porticos and, as at Osterley Park, colonnaded screens, their external differences from the earlier Palladian style are mainly of detail and decoration rather than of structure with an added element of the 'picturesque'. It is in the field of interior decoration that his true genius lay and the glories of Adam country houses are mainly inside — and in colour. Particular artists who worked with him are the painters, Antonio Zucchi (1726-95), Angelica Kauffman (1740-1807), Giovanni Battista Cipriani (1727-85) and the Wedgwood designer, John Flaxman (1755-1826).

Locations

Scotland:

PALLADIAN: **Duff House**, Grampian, 1739, W. Adam (SSS); **Pollok House**, Strathclyde, 1752, Adams; **Floors Castle**, Borders, 1739, Adam, Playfair.
ADAM: **Culzean Castle**, Strathclyde, 1792.
GOTHIC: **Inverary Castle**, Morris, 1760.

England:

North — PALLADIAN: **Dunham Massey**, Cheshire, 1750 (NT); **Ormesby Hall**, Cleveland, 1750 (NT); **Maister House**, Humberside, 1744 (NT); **Nostell Priory**, West Yorkshire, 1733, Paine, Adam (NT).
ADAM: **Newby Hall**, North Yorkshire, 1775.
GOTHIC: **Auckland Castle**, Durham, 1795, Wyatt.
NEO-CLASSICAL: **Heaton Hall**, Greater Manchester, 1772, Wyatt.

Midlands — PALLADIAN: **Melbourne House**, Derbyshire, 1744; **West Wycombe Park**, 1750, Revett (NT); **Claydon House**, Buckinghamshire, 1765 (NT).
ADAM: **Kedleston Hall**, Derbys, 1760, R. Adams; **Moccas Court**, H&W, 1775.
NEO-CLASSICAL: **Berrington Hall**, H&W, 1781, Holland (NT).

East Anglia — PALLADIAN: **Houghton Hall**, Norfolk, 1750, Campbell; **Island Hall**, Cambridgeshire, 1750.
GOTHIC: **Beeston Hall**, Norfolk, 1786.

London — PALLADIAN: **Chiswick House**, Chiswick, 1725, Burlington (EH); **Marble Hill House**, Twickenham, Morris (EH); **Ranger's House**, Blackheath, 1725 (EH).
ADAM: **Osterley Park House**, 1768 (NT); **Kenwood**, 1769 (EH); **Apsley House**, 1778.

Southeast — PALLADIAN: **Basildon Park**, Berkshire, 1776, Carr (NT); **Clandon Park**, Surrey, 1735 (NT); **Hatchlands**, Surrey, 1760 (NT).
GOTHIC: **Mottisfont Abbey**, Hampshire, 1750 (NT).
NEO-CLASSICAL: **Broadlands**, Hampshire, 1792.

Southwest — PALLADIAN: **Pencarrow**, Cornwall, 1750; **Hatch Court**, Somerset, 1755; **Lydiard Mansion,** Wiltshire, 1749, Morris; **Stourhead**, Wiltshire, 1722, Campbell (NT).

Georgian Town Houses

The building of streets of terraced town houses in a range of sizes and grades begun at the end of Queen Anne's reign continued apace throughout the Georgian era. The early London Building Acts had a marked influence throughout the country and in 1774 a fresh act drafted by architects Sir Robert Taylor and George Dance, the younger, came into effect and virtually dictated the design of all urban domestic buildings until well into the next century. It defined seven grades of building according to their volume, cost and location — four of street houses, two of individual houses, and one covering mills and the like. It banned all wooden decorations from facades and required window sash boxes to be concealed behind brickwork. This form of enforced standardisation was the major influence upon the architectural style of Georgian urban housing although individual builders of the day continued to reflect the prevailing fashions of the proliferating pattern books in the design of facades and in added decoration. Not infrequently, especially in the remoter provinces, that interpretation of fashion was somewhat loose and belated — builder's Palladian, speculator's Adam. Another influence was the growing availability of the products of the industrial revolution — typical examples are Coade Stone (1770), a patent composition for mouldings and sculpture, forms of stucco called 'Adams Cement' (1773), decorative ironwork, cast instead of wrought, from firms like Carrons, the cannon makers, and graded and sized Welsh slates.

Above:

Bedford Square, WC1. Plain four-storey houses in yellow brick with ornaments in Coade stone built c1775 and probably designed by Thomas Leverton. Notice the ornamental ironwork, and the balustrading. (The glazing is clearly more recent.)

Terrace housing consisted of several types — rows of identical but individual houses, long terraces of uniform houses, similar terraces designed to give the impression that they are complete buildings in themselves — the so-called 'palace' terrace like the celebrated Royal Crescent in Bath, Bedford Square in London and Charlotte Square in Edinburgh. These grander terraces and even some lesser ones were 'landscaped' in various ways by open spaces and gardens. They also sported the architectural embellishments of current fashion — Palladian pediments and pilasters, Adam porticos and decorations, Green revival entablature.

The main characteristics of Georgian town houses are shown below.

Plan: The plans of the larger individual houses reflected those of fashionable country houses often with elaborate staircases. Those of terraced houses

Above:
Market Place, Blandford Forum, Dorset. The Town Hall (centre) and the houses to its right were rebuilt after the fire of 1734 by John Bastard.

Left:
A Georgian street in Taunton, Somerset, leading up to the church of St Mary Magdalene. The houses are c1788 but early Georgian in style, the apparently 15th century 'perp' church tower was rebuilt in 1858.

Below:
East Side, Fitzroy Square, W1. A palatial terrace by the Adam brothers (1793-98). Notice the round headed windows and the formalised 'rustication' on the ground floor, the fanlights and the simple doorcases, the unfluted Ionic pilasters of the centre pavilion.

became standardised according to grade and ranged from a narrow fronted (12-15ft), 24ft (8m) deep house with two rooms on each floor — kitchen and parlour on ground floor, bedrooms above to much grander establishments — frontages of 32ft (10m) or more with depths of 110ft (32m) running from a basement under the street front back to a mews (stable) block at the rear. In the early and mid-period, most rooms are square but in late Georgian times, many have curved ends and arched niches.

Elevations and Walling: Smaller houses had three storeys only; larger houses often had basements plus four storeys with a two/three-storey mews block. Kitchens and service rooms were in the basement; the dining room and sitting room were on the ground floor; the first floor with its higher ceiling had the drawing room in front, probably a library behind. Other floors had bedrooms with servants' attics at the top. Early houses are faced in red brick with pilasters and cornices, middle period faces are plainer with cornice and string courses only and yellow-brown bricks became more common especially in London. Late period houses have stucco facing marked to look like stone including scoring to simulate rustication of the lower storeys.

Roofing: Shallower pitched roofs became possible with the introduction of Welsh slates in graded stock sizes after c1750 — called after female aristocrats from little 'ladies' (12×8in) to great 'queens' (36×24in).

Chimneys: Chimney breasts are internal and on outside or party walls and with multiple flues ending in chimney pots late in the period.

Windows and Doors: Sash windows prevailed throughout the period with

Left:
This little terrace was probably built in the first decade of the 19th century, but there is no mistaking the early Georgian style. It is in the High Street, Chipping Campden, Gloucestershire.

glazing bars becoming progressively thinner as did sash boxes. The usual pattern is six panes to a sash on larger windows and three in smaller square attic or basement windows. In bigger houses, the tall first floor windows would have 15 panes and open on to a balcony, stonework at first but later in wrought iron with heavy, severe Greek motifs, acanthus, volutes, fret, etc. Some bay windows, segmental or octagonal, begin to appear at the end of the period. The usual door case of the early period had Ionic or Corinthian columns with full entablature under a curved or triangular pediment enclosing a full eight panelled door. Later on, columns became slimmer, pediments were either broken or open and the door was surmounted by a fanlight at first of simple design. Late in the period, the Adam influence brought in very slim pilasters with typical drop decoration and the celebrated Adam-style fanlight under a plain brick arch.

Interiors: Early in the period rooms tended to be panelled with a distinctive dado rail; after about 1760, panelling was confined to below the dado rail with wall-papering or colour wash above; later still, the panelling disappeared and the dado line was painted on to a colour washed wall — especially in 'Adam' colours relieved by a frieze of Adam relief ornaments mass-produced for use by the building trade. Similarly ceilings began plain with simple cornices and progressed to the embroidered Adam style. Chimney pieces began with pilasters running up to consoles under the cornice and ended with carved marble or painted wood 'Adam style' fire-surrounds and mantelpieces like those fashionable again today.

Fig 29
Adam style decoration — summed up in a single fanlight design.

The Regency Period, c1790-1840

The term 'Regency' has much wider connotations than a quirk in monarchical succession. Factually the Regency lasted only from 1811 when George III became sufficiently deranged for his son to be appointed Regent and 1820 when the king died and the Regent became George IV. His standing as a monarch may be low but his wit and intelligence and above all his great taste and understanding in all matters artistic are beyond doubt and he exercised great influence, even as Prince of Wales, among creative artists in all fields. In terms of style and *mores* the Regency period thus runs from the last decade of the 18th century until the first decade of Victoria's reign. It was in essence the period of rustic calm that preceded the upheavals of the Industrial Revolution when three-quarters of the population still lived in villages and small towns and made their livelihoods on or out of the land. Even that population was only nine million in 1801 but had reached 14 million in 1831 and 20 million in 1851. Upper and middle-class Britain of the Regency period

Below left:
Soane's Museum, Lincoln's Inn. The spirit of the age 'elegant but light-hearted frivolity'. This rather whimsical facade to a standard Georgian London house is by the great Classical architect, 1812-34.

Below right:
Some aspects of the Greek Revival confirmed the pagan nature of Classical architecture in the minds of the early 19th century sceptics. An example is the use of these caryatids copied from the Erectheum, Athens on St Pancras' Church, Euston Road, NW1, 1819-22, by H. W. and W. Inwood.

was also immensely prosperous, self-confident, accustomed to success and seemingly possessed at all levels of society with an almost tireless energy. The defeat of Napoleon and the avoidance of the infection of the French Revolution had in effect made the British the 'lords of the Earth'. The main source of national wealth was the land — during the Napoleonic wars, agricultural production had increased 20-fold — and the landed gentry were richer than they had ever been before or have been since. As John Lambton, first Earl of Durham, put it in 1821 '£40,000 a year, a moderate income — such a one that a man might jog with' — and income tax was abolished in 1815 and did not return until 1842.

A great deal of this wealth was, happily, returned to the countryside and to a lesser extent to the cities and towns. Britain was never to be so beautiful again. Massive houses were built all over the country as well as a host of smaller houses, farm houses, workers' cottages — generally stylish and in good materials with excellent workmanship. Barns built at the time were, it is said, meant to last for centuries. Those cities that did benefit from the building boom achieved a new almost startling elegance — London, of course, but a contemporary writer describes another with its tasteful Grecian buildings, fine residences and clean broad streets as 'the most beautiful town in England after London'. He was describing not Bath or Cheltenham but *Liverpool*. In fact most major towns and cities, and especially seaports — Bristol, Newcastle, Dundee, Glasgow, Manchester, Perth, Edinburgh — saw considerable new building during the period. Isolation from Continental watering places during the Napoleonic wars also brought about the flowering of the English inland spas and seaside resorts. As a result, places like Brighton, Hastings, Cheltenham, and Leamington grew from small villages to sizeable towns within a few decades.

The prevailing influence throughout the period was that of the 'Picturesque' — making nature conform to art by landscaping on a grand scale and building follies and romantic ruins to improve the prospect. In the towns the aim was to achieve *rus in urbe* — town dwellings giving the impression from within and without of being in the country — houses built in parks and looking out on trees and gardens. As far as architectural styles are concerned, the Greek Revival of the late Georgian period predominated from about 1810 onwards until c1830 when there was a reversion to Italianate styles and the Gothic Revival also began in earnest. Though the Gothic style had never died out completely, in the 18th century it was confined largely to the remodelling of medieval buildings, for garden ornaments and follies and for a few maverick houses like Walpole's famous Strawberry Hill. In the early 19th century it began to gain new intellectual acceptance. There were three main factors.

First was the 'Romantic' movement inspired by the widely-read novels of Sir Walter Scott (1771-1832) — *Ivanhoe, Kenilworth, et al*. The second was a re-examination of Gothic architecture itself by scholars like Thomas Rickman (1776-1841) who classified the Gothic styles into 'Norman', 'Early English', 'dec' and 'perp'. Finally there were the passionate polemics of Pugin — Augustus Welby Northmore Pugin (1812-1852) who saw classical architecture as 'pagan' and the Gothic the only suitable style for churches.

The Regency period thus ended in a clash of the major styles — Classical versus Gothic and the advocates of the latter scored a second major advance in its adoption in neo-Perpendicular form for the Houses of Parliament in 1835, the first having been Jeffrey Wyatville's romantic rebuilding of Windsor Castle for George IV. Significantly, the architect for the Houses of Parliament was Sir James Barry (1795-1860) whose reputation was based primarily on classical and Italianate buildings. His assistant was Pugin who was responsible for the decoration and between them they achieved a building that blended together both styles — the symmetry of the classical ground plan with the asymmetric skyline of the Gothic. As Pugin put it: 'All Grecian, Sir; Tudor details on a classic body.' It was a fitting herald to the Victorian period that was to follow.

Below:
Impetus to the Gothic Revival was given by Wyatville's rebuilding of Windsor Castle, 1820-30. This is St George's Gate and the south range. He not only added battlements and dummy machicolations, he also cut grooves in the freestone blocks to give the impression of regular masonry.

Regency Town Houses and Villas

The Regency period is distinguished by a series of elegant town planning schemes which in the manner of the London Building Acts produced separate houses — now called 'villas', streets of houses, separate, semi-detached and in terraces of varying sizes and grades. Architects, now members of a fully fledged profession, at least in England, created the designs and these were executed by a new breed of entrepreneur, the building contractor. The architect who epitomises the period was John Nash (1752-1835), the arch-exponent of the Picturesque whose greatest work was the design for the lay-out of Regent's Park and Regent Street in London from 1811 onwards. (He worked closely with Humphrey Repton (1752-1818), the landscape gardener.) His successors in London were Decimus Burton (1800-1881) and Thomas Cubitt (1788-1855), the prototype of the modern 'developer'. In Edinburgh, the architects who helped to create 'The Athens of the North' were Robert Reid (1774-1856), Archibald Elliot (1761-1823) and William Henry Playfair (1790-1857). Newcastle's Grecian centre was designed by John Dobson (1787-1865) and laid out by the developer, Richard Grainger (1797-1861). Cheltenham was largely built to the designs of John Buonarroti Papworth (1775-1847) and the brothers Robert and Charles Jearrad. Brighton

Left:
Carlton House Terraces, The Mall, SW1. The almost triumphal epitome of the Greek Revival stuccoed Regency terrace, this is the southern one of the pair built by Nash between 1827-32. It is 460ft (140m) long and mounted on a platform supported by Doric columns made of cast iron.

Above:
Perhaps the most distinguished Classical building in London in the Greek Revival style is, appropriately, The Athenaeum, Pall Mall, SW1. It was built 1828-30 by Decimus Burton.

and Hove, so beloved of the Regent himself, were planned by Charles Augustus Busby (1788-1834).

Like building itself, style in the Regency period became more speculative. Although the Greek Revival style predominates in a Regency town like Cheltenham, nonetheless there are numerous pleasing individual houses and terraces where the style is Gothic, Italianate or even Oriental. Style is once again used as a form of decoration but applied to houses that retain the essential symmetry, compactness and liveable layout of the Georgian period. What gives the Regency period its flavour is an unmistakable air of elegant but light-hearted frivolity. These are the main characteristics of Regency town houses.

Plan: The Georgian rectangular plan is still retained in general but many front walls are formed into shallow curved bays.

Elevation and Walling: The arrangement of floor heights — the first floor deeper than the rest — is retained as is the gradation of window sizes. Most

Above:
***'Rus in urbe'* — the country in the town — on the grand scale is this Greek Revival country house in the middle of Cheltenham, the Queen's Hotel, built 1838 by the Jearrad brothers and copied for railway hotels all over the country in the next decade.**

faces are plain up to the third storey where there is a deep coved string course with third storey windows and coved parapet above. In individual houses broad overhanging eaves are not unusual. Some pilasters are still seen between houses or at the end of blocks as are some central pediments. First floor windows open on to cast iron balconies some with canopies shaped like Chinese pagodas. Iron work — canopies, railings, boot scrapers, etc are all cast iron. Regency balconies are light and decorated with motives of vines, scrolls, flowers, etc. Walling is of brick but is stuccoed with 'Roman Cement' to look like stone. (Walls were not coloured in the Regency period, this is a later affectation.) The lower storey is etched to resemble rustication.

Roofing: Roofs are still hipped and with a shallow pitch and tiled with mass-produced Welsh slates.

Chimneys: Plain brick stacks with tallish pots are positioned on outside walls.

Windows and Doors: The majority of windows are still rectangular, sashed with multiple panes but more segmental or hexagonal bays often running from the ground to the eaves are seen and the 'French' window comes into vogue. In the lower storeys, window openings are sometimes rounded or segmented with etched-in keystones and voussoirs. Pointed window arches are found in Gothic style houses and all styles often have margin lights — a narrow strip of glass held by narrow glazing bars round the periphery of a window. Entrance doors are rather plain with square or semi-circular fanlights. Doorcases are also usually simple although classic porches, some with balconies, are found in villas.

Interiors: Interior decoration reflected the style of the house and was predominantly Greek Revival with overtones of the 'French Empire' style, the Gothic and touches of Egyptian, Chinese and Indian motives. The Regency style extended to furniture as well as interior decoration and women's clothes. Despite the profusion of modes, good taste made graceful and elegant what might have been — and was later to become — disastrously flamboyant.

Above:
But the change to Gothick was already under way — battlements, bracket moulds, traceried windows, pinnacles and the oriel window, Oriel Lodge, Cheltenham, was built c1825.

Left:
The Italianate style came in at the end of the Regency period. Here is an example complete with flat-topped campanile — Cornerways, The Park, Cheltenham. It was built c1840 and the architect was probably S. W. Daukes.

Regency Country Houses

The wealth of the upper classes in the Regency period found expression in a boom in the building of country houses and in modernising those of earlier times. There was no shortage of land, of money, of architects or of building styles — and since this abundant situation prevailed until the outbreak of World War 1, one should add that during the Regency, restraint and good taste were not yet in the short supply that both were to become later. If there was a prevailing fashion it was for the 'Picturesque' — the influence of the works of Claude Lorraine and Nicholas Poussin was still powerful — and to achieve it, Gothic was as effective as Greek Revival especially if landscape gardeners like Humphrey Repton were involved. Most architects could adopt either style to meet the wishes of a client — plus few others of a 'Romantic' flavour, Italianate, Tudor, Elizabethan and as at Sezincote in Gloucestershire (1805), what might be called Nabob Moghul. When we come to look at Regency country houses, therefore, the interest lies in identifying the basic

Above:
The Rotunda, Ickworth, Suffolk, an eccentric house for an eccentric nobleman, the much travelled 4th Earl of Bristol whose name was adopted by many hotels in Europe. Begun in 1795 by (?) Francis Sandys, it was not completed until 1830 and by John Field. The frieze is of Coade stone and based on designs by Flaxman. *John Bethell, The National Trust*

Above:
Arlington Court, Devon. In complete contrast to Ickworth, an example of austere Greek Revival by Thomas Lee c1820. The circular porch is in the Greek Doric order, the coupled antae (pilasters) at the corners are undecorated. *Jonathan Gibson, The National Trust*

style and its interpretation by the individual architect. We are now in an era of eclecticism — freely borrowing from any style that pleases and Palladio's rules are far behind us.

The main exponents of the Greek Revival school were Benjamin Henry Latrobe (1764-1820) who emigrated to the United States in 1795 and helped with the Capitol in Washington, Sir Robert Smirke (1780-1867) who designed the British Museum, William Wilkins (1778-1839), George Dance (1741-1825), Charles Robert Cockerell (1788-1863) (son of the builder of Sezincote), Joseph Michael Gandy (1771-1843) as well as Nash, Burton, Papworth and Playfair who were also involved in building towns. In Scotland the style was continued outside the period by Alexander 'Greek' Thompson (1817-75). But each of these architects could and did on occasion produce buildings in other styles.

The Gothick style was dominated throughout the Regency by the remarkable architectural dynasty of the Wyatt family. James Wyatt (1747-1813) was a rival of Adam's and the builder of the Gothic mansion of Ashridge. (He was also known as 'Wyatt the Destroyer' because of his unfeeling restoration work on a number of cathedrals and the precursor of the Victorian 'scrapers'.) His son, Benjamin Dean Wyatt (1775-1850) enlarged Adam's Apsley House, 'No 1, London' for the Duke of Wellington but better known was his nephew Jeffery Wyatt (1766-1840). His masterpiece was Windsor Castle which he remodelled for George IV between 1824 and 1837. He got a knighthood for his work and added 'ville' to his name in the process. 'Veal or mutton' said the king when asked, 'Call yourself what you like'. But the example of Wyatville's Windsor was emulated in castles, country houses and villas throughout the land — an added impetus to the Gothic Revival.

Because of the variety of styles and idiosyncracies of the period, it is not possible to list characteristics of Regency country houses. There are, however, some things in common. The Regency saw the introduction of the country house party — an institution not entirely extinct today — and with it the need for changes in interior designs and lay-outs. The tendency was to put public rooms on the ground floor again, for more attention to be paid to making other rooms, libraries, dining rooms, etc more comfortable and more accessible and for improving domestic facilities. There was also a tendency to build estate buildings in the same style as the main house and this often extended to cottages for estate workers.

Finally, one feature of the Regency period was the *cottage orne*, a product of the cult of the 'Picturesque'. It was usually a rustic cottage of romantic design with barge boards, oriel windows and similar Gothic features, invariably with a thatched roof and built as an ornament to a park, a labourer's home, a lodge or as a week-end retreat. Nash built a village of them at Blaise Hamlet near Bristol in 1811 and Cheltenham's Papworth published a book of designs for them in 1818, *Designs for Rural Residences*.

Locations

Scotland:

Fasque, Grampian, Gothic, 1809; **Blairquhan Castle**, Strathclyde, Tudor-Gothic, 1824, Burn; **Dalmeny House**, Lothian, Tudor-Gothic, 1817, Wilkins.

Wales:

Plas Newydd, Gwynedd, 1797, Wyatt (NT).

England:

North — **Normanby Park**, Humberside, Greek Revival, 1800, Smirke; **Tatton Park**, Cheshire, Neo-Classical, 1825, S. and L. W. Wyatt (NT); **Belsay**, Northumberland, Greek Revival, 1817, Monck (EH).

Midlands — **Althorp**, Northamptonshire, 1790, Holland; **Shugborough**, Staffordshire, Neo-Classical, 1798, Wyatt (NT); **Attringham Park**, Salop, Greek Revival, 1785, Steuart (NT); **Sezincote**, Gloucestershire, Moghul, 1805, Cockerell.

East Anglia — **Ickworth**, Suffolk, 1825, Field (NT).

London — **Gunnersbury Park**, 1802, Smirke; **Soane's Museum**, Lincoln's Inn, 1812, Soane.

Southeast — **Hammerwood Park**, West Sussex, Greek Revival, 1792, Latrobe; **Goodwood House**, West Sussex, Neo-Classical, 1795, Wyatt; **Arundel Castle**, Gothic, 1815, Abraham; **Royal Pavilion**, Brighton, East Sussex, Oriental, 1820, Nash.

Southwest — **Blaise Castle House**, Avon, 1795, Paty, Cockerell; **Blaise Hamlet**, cottages ornées, 1811, Nash; **Claverton Manor**, Avon, Neo-Palladian, 1820, Wyatville; **Arlington Court**, Devon, Greek Revival, 1823, Lee (NT); **Powderham Castle**, Devon, Gothic Revival, 1796, Wyatt.

Above:
Gunnersbury Park, Acton, W6. A partner of Henry Holland, Alexander Copland built this house for himself in 1802. Doric columns and pilasters on the ground floor, round headed and canopied windows on the first and second floors.

Below:
South Range, Windsor Castle. Originally the Norman curtain wall of the castle, this range was rebuilt by Wyatville to house apartments for distinguished visitors. The George IV Gateway in the middle and the ground floor windows are unmistakably Gothic.

The Victorian Period, c1840-1914

This book is concerned with historical buildings not buildings in general so if we define history as the events of a period outside the personal experience of anyone now living, the age of Queen Victoria and her immediate heirs is our most recent 'historical' period and hence the last to be covered. Beginning about 1840 it came to an abrupt and bloody end in the horrors of World War 1 in 1914. It is sufficiently close to us for the perceived vices, virtues and values of its society to be the subject of contemporary political debate and for any discussion of its achievements in music, literature and the arts including, not least, in architecture, to be a matter of high controversy and subject to repeated reassessment and reappraisal from one decade to the next. Compare, for example, the ease with which British Rail were able to pull down the Hardwicks' great Doric arch at Euston station (built 1835-39) in 1961 with the public outcry that would arise were such a thing even contemplated today. Or, further down the scale, observe the value now attached to Victorian urban housing in contrast to the alacrity with which thousands of such houses were demolished in the immediate post-World War 2 era. In short, we cannot make our minds up about the Victorians because, perhaps, it is as yet too early.

As far as Victorian architecture is concerned, the most obvious fact is the quantity of it that has come down to us and is still in use and very much alive — churches, houses, schools and colleges, public buildings and utilities of all kinds. The sheer numbers of such buildings is a reminder of the tremendous growth of population that occurred in the 19th century — from nine million in 1801 to 16 million in 1841 and 32 million in 1901. The population had grown

Left:
The Victorian era encapsulated in a single canopied shrine. Gothic spire, larger-than-life seated figure, marbled sculpture, decorated frieze — the Albert Memorial in Kensington Gardens by Sir George Gilbert Scott, 1863-75.

Right:
The 'battle of the styles' (1). The National Gallery, William Wilkins, completed 1838 in the Classical style.

nearly four times in 100 years whereas over the preceding three centuries it had only just doubled. Moreover, it was a much more mobile population following the development of the railways from the late 1830s onwards and the effects of massive industrial development changed an essentially rural population of 1801 when only 30% lived in towns to one in 1901 when nearly 80% did — and also made it immensely prosperous compared with the standards of the past. Despite the overcrowding of the slums in the great cities, most Victorian families lived in less crowded, more comfortable and more sanitary conditions than had any previous generation. (And even the slums were gaslit.) This factor has an important bearing on the quality of the design of much Victorian urban housing. The need to build prolifically and build quickly made no allowances for an individual customer's discretion and taste — even assuming that he had any. It was enough for most occupants — the majority of them tenants of large property owners — that the houses they were offered were better than any that went before and the devil take the architectural purists. Mass-produced speculative building had arrived and if one type or style was well received it was copied extravagantly and indiscriminately by any builder out for a quick profit and without the benefit of an architect, inevitably deteriorating in taste and quality as it descended the social scale. In short, taste and style were for those who could afford them. But in good taste or not, the Victorians like the generations before them intended their buildings to last — and they have.

In the field of public and major private architecture where the customer could have his say, there was a variety of styles to choose from. There is, in fact, no one Victorian style although there is perhaps one predominant Victorian architectural theme — a romantic involvement with the past that some people call 'historicism'. In domestic and public architecture this meant

making 'new buildings look like old ones' as one authority has put it, something without precedent in earlier times. Innovation in design and the use of new materials — girders of cast iron, wrought iron, and steel, great sheets of plate glass — came in the field of civil engineering — bridges for railways, roads and canals, railway stations, exhibition centres, market halls and glasshouses culminating in the biggest glasshouse of all time — Sir William Paxton's Crystal Palace of 1851. Such new materials and techniques were employed in other public works like prisons and pumping stations but their full exploitation had to wait until the modern era. The mid-century Victorians for the most part not only preferred the past but the past as they imagined it to have been after reading the medieval novels of Sir Walter Scott, Alfred Lord Tennyson's poetic idylls of chivalry or from gazing at pre-Raphaelite visions of a prim and sanitised Middle Ages.

In the field of architecture the period of the early part of Victoria's reign is often described as the time of the 'battle of the styles', of Gothic opposing Classical and a battle which was as much philosophical and religious, even political, as artistic — but all the more fervent for it. Many 19th century savants like Pugin and later, the critic and writer John Ruskin (1819-1900) saw the Gothic as Christian and the Classical as pagan. Others saw English medieval Gothic as a 'national' style fitting for an age of intense nationalism and imperial expansion although, in fact, most architecture exported to the Empire was Classical. But neither side totally prevailed nor did any combined or compromise style emerge. Those who commissioned architects or set up competitions for major projects — another Victorian innovation — chose what suited their purposes best and the architects, now often heading large practices with many assistants, met their wishes in either style. Although one always has the impression that Gothic predominated in the Victorian period, in fact, apart from churches and colleges, the Classical style more than held its own. By about 1870, Gothic was largely confined to ecclesiastical use,

Left:
The 'battle of the styles' (2). The Royal Courts of Justice, The Strand by G. E. Street, 1874-82, Victorian 'High Gothic' at its zenith. It was the last great Gothic building to be built in London and is often known as 'the grave of Gothic'.

Right:
The 'battle of the styles' (3). The Natural History Museum, Cromwell Road, Alfred Waterhouse, 1873-81. 'Streaky-bacon Gothic' — faced with bands of yellow and blue terracotta with charming sculptures of animals as a decoration.

Left:
The battle over — York Railway Offices, 1906, in 'Norman Shaw Queen Anne' by William Bell and Horace Field. It is adorned with almost every architectural device known to the Classical style.
John Shannon

various forms of the Classical were used for public buildings and a revived form of the vernacular, largely Elizabethan and Jacobean, for larger houses — and all rather overdone. We shall examine these styles further in **Victorian Churches** and **Victorian Houses**.

There were, however, voices raised against the more ornate aspects of Victorian design including architecture. William Morris (1834-96) with his arts and crafts movement was inspired by what he perceived as the 'joy of labour' of medieval craftsmen and the belief that art should be by 'the people for the people' rather than for the pleasure of an informed elite. His ideas for better, simpler, two-dimensional designs for houses and all that went into them, and the house he had built — Red House, Bexley Heath — influenced several late Victorian architects and through them affected the course of 20th century building design. In this regard and for his belief in preservation, he was, like Sir William Paxton, rather ahead of his time.

Victorian Churches

The rapid expansion of the population and the development of new industrial towns and villages in the mid-19th century was also accompanied by a powerful revival in religious belief and the building of hundreds of new churches and chapels coupled with the restoration of many hundreds more. All religious denominations were involved — the Anglican church enhancing its heritage, the Roman Catholics and nonconformists enjoying their release from centuries of restriction by new liberal legislation. The established church alone built an average of 100 new churches each year from 1840 to 1900 and these were outnumbered by those built by the other denominations. Churches and chapels come in all shapes and sizes and once again there is no strictly Victorian style or method of building. There are, however, clear themes in design that reflect the changing architectural and religious fashions of the period.

For the Anglicans, there was a powerful movement away from the 'convenient auditory' concept of the Stuart and Georgian periods towards a more medieval and Roman Catholic tradition of the supremacy of the altar and its attendant rituals. In architectural terms this required that the chancel and the nave should be clearly differentiated by a chancel arch and greater decoration of the chancel internally and by separate roofing externally. A porch was required as was a separate vestry (or sacristy). Galleries were no longer acceptable. It goes without saying that this reversion to medieval religious practice also meant a reversion to churches in the Gothic style.

The first churches built in the 19th century Gothic-revival style, both Anglican and Roman Catholic, were usually Perpendicular, often 'perp' Gothic embellishments to what was structurally a compact Classical building. Pugin, a Roman Catholic convert himself, influenced both persuasions with his writings early in Victoria's reign. He looked for genuine medieval structures as well — vaulting, wooden roofs at different levels, asymmetric plans, stained glass, *et al.* He himself designed numerous churches and his work was widely admired. From about 1840 onwards, the popular style was Early English or Lancet but this gave way to a general adoption of the Middle Pointed or Decorated style of the 13th century — and 'decorated' to the Victorians really meant that.

The most important of Pugin's disciples was Sir George Gilbert Scott (1811-78) of whom it was later written that he 'built or interfered with nearly 500 churches, 39 cathedrals and minsters, 25 universities and colleges, and many other buildings besides'. Another was Scott's pupil, George Edmund Street (1824-81). There was also something of a Romanesque revival in the 1840s and this was followed by a Ruskin-inspired adoption of the styles of Venetian Gothic, especially its use of alternating layers of coloured brick or stone — High Victorian Gothic or less reverently, 'streaky bacon Gothic' — which lasted to the 1870s. Its arch exponent was William Butterfield (1814-1900). The later decades of the 19th century saw a return to the simpler styles of the early Gothic period for town churches exemplified in the work of George Frederick Bodley (1827-1907) and in Truro Cathedral by John

Above left:
An early 19th century nonconformist chapel built privately in 1816 in ashlared stone is North Place Chapel, Cheltenham. It is classical in style but with Gothic windows in the upper storey.

Above right:
Christ Church, Cheltenham, 1830-40, Jearrads, is undoubtedly Gothic and obviously 'perp'.

Loughborough Pearson (1817-97). But for their Westminster Cathedral, the Roman Catholics chose a design by John Francis Bentley (1839-1902) which owes more to the Byzantines than to the Goths and has the 'streakiest bacon' in London. It was completed in 1910 and is based on the Hagia Sophia in Istanbul — built 532-537 AD — and emphasises the point that the only common architectural style in the Victorian era was the historic past.

Restoration

The Victorians not only built churches, they also 'restored' them — ruthlessly and the most ruthless 'restorer' was George Gilbert Scott. Few medieval churches escaped the restorers' attentions and until the 1870s when William Morris founded the Society for the Protection of Ancient Buildings (SPAB), 'restoration' meant not preservation but rebuilding and refitting into a style of idealised Gothic that allowed none of the 'untidy' medieval variations in evolving Gothic style to survive without correction. The Victorians knew they knew better than the ancients. To be fair, however, their work — known as 'scraping' — did ensure the survival of many badly neglected medieval churches in danger of falling down.

Nonconformist Churches

Although the various nonconformist denominations continued to build 'auditories' in large numbers in the new industrial areas, they too succumbed in the 1850s to the ethics of 'Christian Gothic' as enunciated by Pugin. Later in the century, like the established church, they also adopted a variety of romantic styles but perhaps with more imagination and flair than the Anglicans. They also kept their galleries and needed no chancels so their churches remained open, light and airy. In Scotland, where the nonconformist Church of Scotland prevailed as the established church, buildings in the Classical style of Alexander 'Greek' Thompson (1817-75) continued to be built until late in the century. Thereafter there were increasing numbers of churches reflecting the Gothic of the High Victorian movement in the south as well as Scotland's own medieval Gothic tradition.

Above:
Holy Trinity, Lyne, Surrey. An Early English and early 'dec' church by Francis, c1849, and the prototype of many Gilbert Scott churches.

Right:
Holy Trinity, Sunningdale, Berkshire. Mainly Early English, the chancel c1860 is by Street, the rest by J. Oldrid Scott (son of Gilbert Scott) and built c1887-88.

Victorian Houses

The Victorian period saw the full flowering of two inextricably linked greatly-loved British institutions — the large country house and social snobbery. The one was killed off largely by the agricultural depression of the 1870s and by death duties introduced in 1894 and the other, though it has survived, was never to be quite as pervasive after 1914. As in previous periods, the style of the large aristocratic country house set the architectural standards of the day which others were happy to follow — from the nouveau riche entrepreneur bent on founding a landed dynasty, to the rich businessman with his detached house in town or in the country, the professional in the *rus in urbe* suburbs served by the new railways, and the carefully graded lower orders in their equally carefully graded semi-detached and terraced houses in the newly built urban estates. The only difficulty was that the bulk of these people had little knowledge or appreciation of architectural style and taste. Those who could afford to employ architects wanted 'a comfortable Gentleman's house in the style of the passing moment'. Those who couldn't took what they could get and were pleased with it but such was the snobbery of the times, once a style had reached the lower orders, it became unacceptable to those higher up. This process of downwards filtration took time, so that by the time the Gothic had reached

Below:
Bear Wood, Sindlesham, Berkshire. An enormous country house on the scale of Blenheim but totally different in style, Bear Wood was built between 1866-1870 by John Walter II, owner of *The Times*. The architect was Robert Kerr. The style can probably be summarised as Jacobean with touches of French-chateaux Gothic. This is the south front. Notice the enormous bay windows and the slanted lights on the stair turret. (Bear Wood is now the Royal Merchant Navy School.)

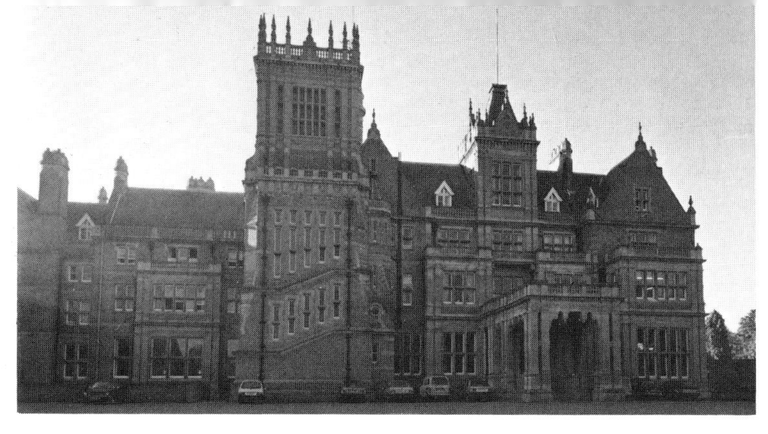

the locally built terraces of Camberwell in 1900, it had generally been out of fashion among architects for 30 years.

In essence Victorian domestic architecture followed a similar pattern to that of the churches not least because most architects designed both churches and houses. We thus have the same proliferation of styles and none that we can analyse in general detail as being typical of the period as we were able to do with the earlier periods. Indeed the great fascination of Victorian houses lies in detecting the bits and pieces of earlier styles — an Elizabethan bay window here, Tudor chimneys there, sash windows set in Gothic arches everywhere. If one wanted to devise some form of test of recognition of historical architectural styles, Victorian houses could hardly be bettered. We shall therefore look at the main styles of grand country houses, large detached houses and urban houses.

Country Houses

Except in Scotland where, as in church architecture the Classical style prevailed until late in the century, the Greek Revival of the Regency period did not last long after 1840. Then there was a brief vogue for a style based on the Italian Renaissance complete with flat topped campanile-type towers and the rambling asymmetry of the Middle Ages. The 'Picturesque' was still sought after and the Victorians were quite successful at achieving it without the need for follies. The influence of Pugin was not confined to churches and early Victorian patricians were soon building or rebuilding in the Gothic style — so Gothic, in fact, that some of Pugin's houses look rather like domesticated cathedrals. Medieval castles too were built but carefully equipped with all the comforts of life that Victorian modernity could bring from water closets to gas lighting. In Scotland, the castle urge took the form of the 'Scottish Baronial' of which the best known example is Balmoral, extended by Prince Albert in the 1850s. And alongside the Gothic were houses based on the more flamboyant of the Elizabethan examples like Woolaton. The final fling of the Gothic and to some extent that of the great country house came in the middle years of Victoria's reign up to about 1875 when the fashion for 'High Victorian Gothic' was at its height. Houses rambled in an orderly, functional way, had spectacular profiles, rich Gothic

Left:
This is the main entrance — almost as forbidding as Caerphilly.

Above:
Albury Park, Surrey. Originally a Tudor house, Albury was remodelled c1700 and again c1800 by Soane and finally by Pugin in 1846-52 — medieval battlemented towers, Tudor turrets and chimneys but rather restrained for Pugin.

Left:
'Hopelessly in love with the Middle Ages', the Marquess of Bute and his architect William Burges transformed Castell Coch, West Glamorgan into an Arthurian-French fantasy castle in 1872.

ornamentation in terra cotta, marble or cast iron and the 'streaky-bacon' use of banded stone and brick. Gothic castles fell out of fashion about the same time and their place was taken by chateaux in the style of the French Renaissance not dissimilar to Scottish Baronial in the plethora of pointed turrets. Generally, the prevailing English style late in the 19th century became Jacobean with Elizabethan bay windows and in Scotland the 'baronial' persisted until the end of the period. After the 1870s, however, country houses steadily became much smaller and the decline of the great country house began.

Among architects whose work will be found in Victorian country houses are Sir Charles Barry, Anthony Salvin (1799-1881) and Pugin for the early period and both Scott and Street also designed houses; Alfred Waterhouse (1830-1905) and Philip Speakman Webb (1831-1915), designer of William Morris's celebrated 'Red House', in the middle 'High Victorian Gothic' period; George Devey (1820-86), William Eden Nesfield (1835-88), and Norman Shaw (1831-1912), Charles Francis Annesley Voysey (1857-1941), both influenced by Morris's ideas, and Sir Edwin Lutyens (1869-1944) at the end of the period. Outstanding Scottish architects for the period were William Burn

(1789-1870), the originator of the 'Scottish Baronial' style, his pupil, David Bryce (1803-76) and the 'Art Noveau' exponent, Charles Rennie Mackintosh (1868-1928).

Detached Houses

Although the great country house was in decline by the end of the 19th century, the large detached house set in its own grounds in the suburbs or in the country continued to thrive and there was a boom in gardens. By 1870, Gothic was no longer fashionable and there was a return to the use of local materials in the simpler styles of the English vernacular of the 16th, 17th and early 18th centuries — not infrequently all in the same building and sometimes with a touch of Scottish baronial as well. The Gothic might be in eclipse but the desire for the Picturesque remained. Norman Shaw was adept at this mixture of styles and his penchant was for Flemish style brickwork, tall chimney stacks with caps, walls tile-hung with shaped tiles — fish scale, etc, sash windows with glazing bars only on the upper sash, plate glass beneath, a plethora of wooden balconies painted white. He was widely imitated. This was the 'Queen Anne Revival' style to its friends, 'Wrenaissance' to its enemies. For smaller houses, the Sussex Wealden house (qv) became his vernacular model. Later, a much simpler and very personalised style of detached house came in with the designs of C. F. A. Voysey — low roughcast walls painted white, steep pitched roofs with wide eaves and dormers, and long mullioned windows. The 'Vernacular Revival' continued to the end of the period with the work of Sir Edwin Lutyens in the traditional style of Surrey. He was later to become the outstanding Classical architect of the early 20th century.

Below left:
A 'domestic cathedral', the former St Pancras Hotel, Euston Road, NW1 (now offices) was built 1868-76 by Sir George Gilbert Scott and is as Gothic as his Albert Memorial, using a similar mixture of materials.

Below right:
On a smaller scale but still vaguely ecclesiastical, Almshouses, Windsor, 1862.

Above:
The Clapham and Wandsworth areas developed in the late 19th century. Illustrated is a two-storey terrace with large bay windows, c1900.

Urban Housing

Detached houses and better class terraces in the larger cities reflected the architectural styles of the day although Georgian-type Classical design with its stuccoed frontages prevailed in London until about 1860. The pattern whereby the rich lived in the country, the better-off in the suburbs and the poor in the inner cities was well established by the mid-19th century. Many of the worst slums occurred in areas where good Georgian houses vacated by the wealthy were let off as rooms to the poor. In other places, such houses were demolished and smaller, often jerry-built terraces were put up in their place. Typical of these are the back-to-back terraces still found in many northern industrial areas. Further up the scale, the Victorian terrace house evolved from the three-storeyed Georgian type with its plain front to the two-storeyed, bay-fronted type built all over the country until World War 1. Bay windows on the first and second floors of terrace houses are very much a Victorian feature as is the back extension which houses the kitchen, wash house and outside lavatory on the ground floor and a spare bedroom and a bathroom on the first. Variations in size and style of this basic type are to be found everywhere, the decoration depending upon the date high fashion reached the area, the locality or the builder. In the suburbs and in some parts of cities, the semi-detached house became fashionable from about 1840 onwards. Two other Victorian innovations of interest are the 'salubrious suburb' of which Norman Shaw's Bedford Park in Acton, London (1876) is the best example, and the 'garden city' — Letchworth in Hertfordshire, begun in 1903 was the first with cottages designed by Voysey. Some Victorian industrialists also continued with schemes for building estate villages for their workers first introduced by Richard Arkwright and Robert Owen around 1800. Of these estates, one of the best is Saltaire near Bradford; others are Port Sunlight and Bourneville.

Locations

We are still surrounded by Victorian housing of all types and the following are only a few of the larger trend-setting houses which are open to the public.

Scotland:

SCOTTISH BARONIAL: **Balmoral Castle**, Grampian, 1851, Prince Albert, W. Smith; **Gosford House**, Lothian, 1883, W. Young; **Torosay Castle**, Strathclyde, 1840, Bryce.
URBAN: **Tenement House**, Glasgow, 1892 (NTS).
MODERN BARONIAL: **The Hill House**, Strathclyde, 1904, C. R. Mackintosh (NTS).

England:

North — TRADITIONAL: **Arley Hall**, Cheshire, 1854, W. White, Jacobean; **Cragside House**, Northumberland, 1885, Shaw (NT).
GOTHIC: **Carlton Towers**, Humberside 1874, Pugin.

Midlands — GOTHIC: **Knebworth House**, Hertfordshire, 1843, Lytton.
JACOBEAN: **Hughenden Manor**, Buckinghamshire, 1847, Lamb (NT).
ITALIAN RENAISSANCE: **Cliveden**, Buckinghamshire, 1851, Barry (NT).
CHATEAU: **Waddesdon Manor**, Buckinghamshire, 1885 (NT).
ARTS & CRAFTS: **Wightwick Manor**, West Midlands, 1887 (NT).

East Anglia — JACOBEAN: **Somerleyton Hall**, Suffolk, 1844, Thomas.

Southeast — GOTHIC: **Albury Park**, Surrey, 1847, Pugin.
TRADITIONAL: **Standen**, West Sussex, 1894, Webb (NT).
NEO-WREN: **Stansted House**, 1900, Blomfield.
VERNACULAR: **Greathead Manor**, Surrey, 1868, Kerr; **Polesden Lacey**, Surrey, 1906, Poynter (NT).

Southwest — ITALIANATE: **Osborne House**, Isle of Wight, 1845, Cubitt.
GOTHIC: **Dunster Castle**, Somerset, 1850, Salvin (NT); **Knightshayes Court**, Devon, 1871, Burges (NT); **Castle Drogo**, Devon 1910, Lutyens (NT).

Below:
The massive apartment block was a Victorian innovation. This mixture of Classical and streaky-bacon Gothic is Albert Court, SW7, 1890.

Bibliography

Reference Books

For anyone wishing to increase their knowledge of historical architecture there are many thousands of reference books on building types and building styles. The following is a list of titles I have found interesting and useful and can recommend. There are, however, some books that are an essential part of any building enthusiast's library. They are:

Fleming, Honour, Pevsner; *Penguin Dictionary of Architecture*; Penguin, 1984.

Nikolaus Pevsner (Ed); *The Buildings of England* (47 volumes); Penguin, various dates. A series in volumes for each county and covering almost every worthwhile building in each town, village or hamlet. *The Buildings of Wales* series has just started with a volume on Powys. *The Buildings of Scotland*, volumes on Lothian and Edinburgh to date.

Alec Clifton-Taylor; *The Pattern of English Building*; Faber, 1980.

John Summerson; *The Classical Language of Architecture*; Thames & Hudson, 1978.

R. W. Brunskill; *Vernacular Architecture*; Faber, 1979.

General

J. Gloag; *Men & Buildings*; Chantry, 1950.

Peter Kidson and Peter Murray; *A History of Architecture*; Harrap, 1962.

Christopher Trent; *England in Brick & Stone*; Blond, 1960.

Hubert Pragnell; *The Styles of English Architecture*; Batsford, 1984.

George Balcombe; *Mitchell's History of Building*; Batsford, 1985.

John G. Dunbar; *The Architecture of Scotland*; Batsford, 1978.

John B. Hilling; *The Historic Architecture of Wales*; University of Wales, 1976.

E. Jones and C. Woodward; *The Architecture of London*; Weidenfeld, 1983.

Churches

J. Betjeman (Ed); *Collins Guide to English Parish Churches*; Collins, 1954.

B. A. Bax; *The English Parsonage*; Murray, 1964.

Hugh Braun; *Parish Churches*; Faber, 1974.

Alec Clifton-Taylor; *English Parish Churches*; Batsford, 1974.

G. H. Cook; *The English Cathedral*; Phoenix, 1960.

Castles

Paul Johnson; *The National Trust Book of British Castles*; Weidenfeld, 1978.

Houses

C. Aslet and A. Powers; *The NT Book of the English House*; Viking, 1985.

Lyndon F. Cave; *The Smaller English House*; Robert Hale, 1981.

Woodforde; *Georgian Houses for All*; RKP, 1978.

J. Mordaunt Crook; *The Greek Revival*; Murray, 1972.
Stefan Muthesius; *The English Terraced House*; Yale University, 1982.

Vernacular and Timber-Framed

R. W. Brunskill; *Timber Building in Britain*; Gollancz, 1985.

Historic Periods

James Lees-Milne; *Tudor Renaissance*; Batsford, 1951.
Kerry Downes; *The Architecture of Wren*; Granada, 1982.
The Buildings of Britain; Series Editor, Alastair Service; *Anglo Saxon & Norman*, Alastair Service, 1982; *Tudor & Jacobean*, Malcolm Airs, 1982; *Stuart & Baroque*, Richard Morrice, 1982; *Regency*, David Watkin, 1982; Barrie & Jenkins.
Dan Cruickshank; *A Guide to the Georgian Buildings of Britain & Ireland*; Weidenfeld, 1985.
R. Dixon and S. Muthesius; *Victorian Architecture*; Thames & Hudson, 1978.

Societies Involved in Historic Buildings and their Preservation

Apart from many smaller and local groups devoted to the study and care of historic buildings there are a number of national bodies of interest to the enthusiast. The main ones are:

The National Trust for Places of Historic Interest or Natural Beauty. Headquarters, 36 Queen Anne's Gate, London SW1H 9AS.
The National Trust for Scotland, 5 Charlotte Square, Edinburgh EH2 4DU.
English Heritage, PO Box 43, Ruislip, Middlesex HA4 0XW.
Historic Buildings & Monuments of Scotland, SDD, Box 157, Edinburgh EH3 7QD.
Cadw: Welsh Historic Monuments, Brunel House, 2 Fitzalan Road, Cardiff CF2 1UY.
The Society of Architectural Historians of Great Britain, c/o Room 208, Chesham House, 30 Warwick Street, London W1R 6AB.
The Georgian Group, 37 Spital Square, London E1 6DY.
The Victorian Society of Great Britain, 1 Priory Gardens, London W4.
The Vernacular Architecture Group, Secretary, Dr N. W. Alcock, 18 Portland Place, Leamington Spa, Warwickshire CV32 5EU.
The Society for the Protection of Ancient Buildings, 37 Spital Square, London E1 6DY.

Index